The *Gifts* of the *Spirit*

TITLES BY *Derek Prince*

Appointment in Jerusalem
(with Lydia Prince)
Derek Prince on Experiencing God's Power
Does Your Tongue Need Healing?
Entering the Presence of God
Faith to Live By
Fasting
The Gifts of the Spirit
God's Medicine Bottle
God's Plan for Your Money
God's Remedy for Rejection
God's Will for Your Life
The Grace of Yielding
The Holy Spirit in You
How to Fast Successfully
Judging: When? Why? How?
Lucifer Exposed
Marriage Covenant
Protection from Deception
Receiving God's Best
Rediscovering God's Church
Self-Study Bible Course, Basic Edition
Self-Study Bible Course, Expanded Edition
Shaping History through Prayer and Fasting
Spiritual Warfare
You Shall Receive Power

The Gifts of the Spirit

Understanding and Receiving God's Supernatural Power in Your Life

Derek Prince

WHITAKER
HOUSE

THE GIFTS OF THE SPIRIT:
Understanding and Receiving God's Supernatural Power in Your Life

Derek Prince Ministries
P.O. Box 19501
Charlotte, North Carolina 28219
www.derekprince.org

ISBN-13: 978-0-88368-291-3
ISBN-10: 0-88368-291-5
Printed in the United States of America
© 2007 by Derek Prince Ministries, International

Whitaker House
1030 Hunt Valley Circle
New Kensington, PA 15068
www.whitakerhouse.com

Library of Congress Cataloging-in-Publication Data
Prince, Derek.
The gifts of the spirit : understanding and receiving God's supernatural power in your life / Derek Prince.
p. cm.
Summary: "Explores the nature and operation of the nine gifts of the Holy Spirit listed by the apostle Paul in 1 Corinthians 12"—Provided by publisher.
ISBN 978-0-88368-291-3 (trade pbk. : alk. paper) 1. Gifts, Spiritual. I. Title.
BT767.3.P75 2007
234'.13—dc22   2007015559

4 5 6 7 8 9 10 11 12 **W** 14 13 12 11 10 09 08

Contents

Part 1:
The Nature of the Gifts

1. The Gifts of the Holy Spirit 8
2. Charisma: Grace Gifts 25
3. The Manifestation of the Spirit 40

Part 2:
Gifts of Revelation

4. A Word of Wisdom 52
5. A Word of Knowledge 73
6. Discernings of Spirits 85

Part 3:
Gifts of Power

7. Faith 106
8. Gifts of Healings 128
9. Workings of Miracles 139

Part 4:
The Vocal Gifts

10. Kinds of Tongues and Interpretation of Tongues 154
11. Prophecy 176
12. How to Judge Prophecy 198

Part 5:
Using the Gifts

13. How to Exercise Spiritual Gifts........................... 224

About the Author 251

PART 1

THE NATURE OF THE *Gifts*

CHAPTER 1

THE *Gifts* OF THE HOLY SPIRIT

T he New Testament depicts Christianity as a supernatural way of life. To be functioning members of the body of Christ, as well as more effective witnesses for Him in the world, we need an understanding of the nine supernatural gifts of the Holy Spirit and their operation in our lives. The apostle Paul listed these gifts in 1 Corinthians 12:

> *There are diversities of gifts, but the same Spirit. There are differences of ministries, but the same Lord. And there are diversities of activities, but it is the same God who works all in all. But the manifestation of the Spirit is given to each one for the profit of all: for to one is given the word of wisdom through the Spirit, to another the word of knowledge through the same Spirit, to another faith by the same Spirit, to another gifts of healings by the same Spirit, to another the working of miracles, to another prophecy, to another discerning of spirits, to another different kinds of tongues, to another the interpretation of tongues. But one and the same Spirit works all these things, distributing to each one individually as He wills.*
>
> (1 Corinthians 12:4–11)

These gifts are all supernatural. None of them could be explained by natural talent, education, or ability. A word of wisdom or knowledge is not the kind of wisdom or knowledge that comes from spending fifteen years in college and having three degrees. It is wisdom or knowledge that is given by the Holy Spirit. Healing is not the type of healing that is administered by the general physician or the surgeon—though we respect medical science and are grateful for it. This is supernatural healing.

THE NINE GIFTS OF THE SPIRIT

Let us look at a more literal translation of some of the gifts of the Spirit from the above passage to prepare us for exploring each of them in some detail in coming chapters. In verse eight, where the *New King James Version* reads, *"For to one is given the word of wisdom through the Spirit, to another the word of knowledge through the same Spirit,"* there is actually no "the" in the Greek. I therefore translate these gifts as *"a* word of wisdom" and *"a* word of knowledge." In verse ten, *"to another the working of miracles"* is literally "working*s* of miracles." Both significant words are plural. Likewise, *"discerning of spirits"* should be "discerning*s* of spirits."

Christianity is a supernatural way of life.

Four of the gifts are therefore plural in nature: (1) gifts of healings, (2) workings of miracles, (3) discernings of spirits, and (4) kinds of tongues. Recognizing the plural nature of these gifts is important for understanding how they function.

The nine gifts are readily divided into three groups of three, under the headings of Revelation Gifts, Power Gifts, and Vocal Gifts.

Revelation Gifts

a word of wisdom

a word of knowledge

discernings of spirits

Power Gifts

faith

gifts of healings

workings of miracles

Vocal Gifts

different kinds of tongues

interpretation of tongues

prophecy

For many years, Bible teachers and commentators have listed the spiritual gifts in groups of three for the purpose of easy reference and classification—three groups, with each group containing three gifts or manifestations. This particular grouping is not the only way we can view the gifts, but it is a useful way to arrange them and helps us to understand them more clearly.

A word of wisdom, a word of knowledge, and discernings of spirits are revelation gifts; they convey revelation we could not receive in any other way. Faith, gifts of healings, and workings of miracles are gifts of power—they get things done. They could also be called dramatic gifts; they are the gifts that really arrest people's attention. Different kinds of tongues, the interpretation of tongues, and prophecy are vocal gifts because they necessarily operate through human vocal cords.

MINISTRY GIFTS AND SPIRITUAL GIFTS

To avoid potential confusion, it is important to consider the relationship and differences between the ministry gifts, which are found in Ephesians 4:11, and these nine gifts of the Holy Spirit.

The context for the gifts mentioned in Ephesians 4:11 is the resurrected Christ, for we read in verses eight and ten: *"'He ascended on high, He led captivity captive, and gave gifts to men.'…He who descended is also the One who ascended far above all the heavens, that He might fill all things."* Verse eleven specifies five main gifts the resurrected Christ gave to humanity: *"He Himself gave some to be apostles, some prophets, some evangelists, and some pastors and teachers."*

Let us look at the gifts in two parallel columns:

Ministry Gifts	The Gifts of the Spirit
Apostles	a word of wisdom
Prophets	a word of knowledge
Evangelists	faith
Pastors	gifts of healings
Teachers	workings of miracles
	prophecy
	discernings of spirits
	different kinds of tongues
	the interpretation of tongues

These two groups of gifts are distinguished from one another in three ways.

The Person as Gift/The Gift Given to a Person

First, with the ministry gifts, the believer himself is the gift given by Christ to His church. The wording emphasizes this: *"He Himself gave some to be apostles...."* He did not give to some "apostleship," but He gave some *to be* apostles. Apostles, prophets, evangelists, pastors, and teachers are Jesus' ministry gifts to His church because the church can never be what He intends without them. For example, the apostle Paul was Jesus' gift to the Gentile believers.

Supernatural gifts are brief, dramatic, arresting manifestations.

In contrast, with spiritual gifts, the gift is given to the person, who is then able to minister it to others. Paul wrote, *"To one is given the word of wisdom through the Spirit, to another the word of knowledge through the same Spirit..."* (1 Corinthians 12:8). Therefore, with ministry gifts, the person *is* the gift, and with spiritual gifts, the person *has* the gift.

The Gift as Lifework/The Gift as Brief Manifestation

Second, with a ministry gift, every aspect of the total ministry makes up the gift. It is like an athlete who runs the mile faster than anybody else. His whole life centers on running the mile. Similarly, for the person who is a ministry gift to the church, his whole life centers on being an apostle, prophet, evangelist, pastor, or teacher. Paul often compared Christian ministry to the activities of athletes because there is so much that is parallel between them in terms of the need for training, discipline, and dedication. A ministry is a lifework.

On the other hand, the nine supernatural gifts are brief, dramatic, brilliant, arresting manifestations that happen and are finished. For instance, a prophetic utterance may last seconds or minutes, and it is complete. It is not something that goes on all the time. A word of wisdom occurs in a few seconds. A man suddenly gets a revelation that directs him to do something that he could not have known to do by natural understanding. When the gift of discernings of spirits is given, a person may suddenly see there is a spirit of pride or lust in someone. The spiritual gift is almost like a flash of lightning or a thunderclap. It is there, and then it is finished.

Character Essential/Character Not a Prerequisite

Third, a ministry gift cannot be divorced from a person's character. It has to be so because of the very nature of ministry gifts; it is essential to their outworking. On the other hand, with spiritual gifts, character is not necessarily involved. It seems as if it should be, but this is not always so. It is important for us to learn this or we will be headed for bitter disappointment. Sometimes, people's faith is even harmed when they meet someone whose character does not seem to match the gift he is exercising.

For example, if a person is lazy and irresponsible before he receives a spiritual gift, he may be just as lazy and irresponsible after receiving the gift. He may stand up and prophesy like an angel, yet keep you waiting for every appointment he ever makes with you. While Paul wrote in Ephesians 4:11, "[Christ] *Himself gave some to be...prophets,*" he also wrote in 1 Corinthians 14:31, "*For you can all prophesy one by one, that all may learn and all may be encouraged.*" All believers may exercise the spiritual gift of prophecy. Yet God never says we will all be prophets. Prophesying, in itself, does not give you the ministry of a prophet, nor the character that necessarily corresponds with a ministry gift. However, if you receive a supernatural gift, it does increase your responsibility. And a responsible person will conduct himself in such a way that the gift will go together with the rest of what he does. What we find is that not all who receive a gift take that responsibility or are mature enough in that way.

To help us understand this concept better, the gifts of the Holy Spirit are like presents under a Christmas tree. It does not take long to put a gift under a Christmas tree or to open a gift. These are momentary acts. I once opened a Christmas present and found I had received an electric shoe polisher, but it did not make me a different person from what I was before I received the shoe polisher. It didn't change any part of my character.

Receiving a supernatural gift increases your responsibility.

Please do not misunderstand me. It is certainly not my purpose to belittle gifts. My purpose is only to point out the differences between various ways through which the grace of God (His free and unmerited favor) and the Holy Spirit operate, as well as their parameters. If we think merely exercising a spiritual gift makes a person spiritual, we should remember Balaam's donkey. This will bring us down to earth again. God made a donkey talk to the prophet because the prophet would not listen to God. (See Numbers 22:22–40.) The lesson can be summarized in this way: If you were a donkey before you prophesied, do you know what you will be afterward? Spiritual gifts alone do not change nature or character. God can use a donkey as a last resort. Again, this does not belittle the gifts, but we must realize they are gifts.

The Gifts and Fruit of the Spirit

Another way to look at gifts and character is to realize spiritual gifts are one thing, and spiritual fruit are another. We have seen there are nine gifts of the Spirit, and Galatians 5:22–23 reveals there are also nine forms of the fruit of the Spirit: *"The fruit of the Spirit is love, joy, peace, longsuffering, kindness, goodness, faithfulness ["faith" KJV], gentleness, self-control."* Many Christians lose out on what God has for them in some measure by failing to make a very basic, logical distinction between the gifts and the fruit of the Spirit. I said earlier the gifts are like presents under a Christmas tree. We can also say the difference between the gifts and the fruit is like the difference between ornaments on a Christmas tree and fruit on a fruit tree. Putting an ornament on a Christmas tree just takes a moment, and the ornament is not actually a part of the tree. Yet you can't place an apple on an apple tree. It arrives by a process of cultivation, growth, and maturation. You know it is going to take a considerable period of time for that apple tree to bear apples that are worth eating. Similarly, there is a process involved with the growth of spiritual fruit. It has to be cultivated by labor, patience, and skill.

It would be absurd to expect a ready-made apple or orange on a tree. The apostle Paul wrote, *"The hard-working farmer must be first to partake of the crops"* (2 Timothy 2:6). Fruit does not come forth without labor. I think this is a fact we often overlook. We speak about fruit growing spontaneously without effort. Fruit can grow on its own, but in the world markets today you could not possibly market any kind of fruit that was simply left to grow by itself. All fruit requires very careful and often intensive cultivation that involves time and care. Similarly, no one will bring spiritual fruit to perfection who does not cultivate it. We should also realize that a gift of the Spirit will not be as effective as it should be unless the fruit of the Spirit is cultivated alongside it. And *exercising* the gift may produce a change in character, even though receiving it does not.

One evidence we are pursuing love is our desire for spiritual gifts.

In 1 Corinthians 13:1–2, Paul pointed out that having all gifts of the Spirit without love is of no value to the person who has them. His statements are very interesting because the gifts may still be valuable to somebody else. If I have the gift of healing and I exercise it without love, it doesn't profit me anything, but it may profit the person who gets healed. Oral Roberts related an incident about this I have never forgotten. A woman was bothering him after a meeting. She was overstepping her bounds and running after him. He told her, "The meeting is closed. I don't pray for people privately." She stuck to him so long that, eventually, in a fit of impatience, he put out his hand and touched her—and she was healed. Even though she was healed, he said, "I got no blessing from it; it didn't profit me anything." The one who exercises the gift does not profit from it unless it is exercised in love. I have had similar experiences at times. I have been surprised at the results, considering how I felt! But God is greater than we are.

Some people say they do not need gifts because they have spiritual fruit. Experience has taught me to question just how much fruit people have who talk like that. Suppose someone says, "I have love; I don't need gifts." This is totally unscriptural because the Bible says, *"Pursue love, and desire spiritual gifts"* (1 Corinthians 14:1). One of the evidences we are pursuing love is that we are desiring the spiritual gifts. In fact, spiritual gifts are the tools by which love works. The gifts are the means by which love is made effective. Love without the gifts is left largely impotent and frustrated. I am sure that love will never lead a believer to refuse God's gifts. My reply to such as person would be, "What are you going to do with all your love? How are you going to help humanity with it? You need the gifts for that." Imagine a mother sitting by her sick child and saying, "Honey, I love you, but I'm just going to sit here. I'm not going to check your temperature, I'm not going to give you medicine, I'm not going to call the doctor, and I'm not even going to pray for you. But I love you." How much love does that mother really have? She has love in word but not in deed.

Again, one of the main means by which love is enabled to act is by the gifts of the Holy Spirit. For instance, if we want to edify the church because we love the church, then we will desire the gift that most edifies the church, which is prophecy. Or, if we love the sick, we will desire the gifts that will enable us to minister to the sick, which are gifts of healings and workings of miracles. Biblical love is always very practical. It does not sit around using nice phrases; it does something.

We must not be one-sided. We need both gifts and love. We need both gifts and fruit. We need both spiritual gifts and ministry gifts. None of these is a substitute for any of the others. We need all of them.

All Believers Have Spiritual Gifts

As we continue to explore the nature of spiritual gifts, I would like to address certain perspectives people have about spiritual gifts that are confusing and unscriptural. The first is that some people believe it is wrong to talk about believers "having" spiritual gifts, as if this indicates pride. Yet a person has nothing to be prideful about when he has received a gift. In the first place, as we have seen, it does not make him any different from what he was before he received it. Second, he has nothing that makes him any different from anybody else except the gift, and it is not something that came from him or that he went out and obtained. A person can have a gift and be grateful for it without being prideful about it.

Second, some people do not think believers should say, for example, "I have a gift of healing." They think if someone is healed, the person who was healed received the gift. Or if prophecy is manifested, they think the recipient obtained the gift. This perspective can have a very confusing effect on people, and I want to point out that it is not really scriptural. If God gives you or me a gift, we have an obligation to confess that He has given it. I know men who obviously have a divine gift of healing but who, in order to avoid controversy or criticism, will not own up to it. They say, "I've never claimed to have a gift of healing. God heals." It is true that God heals, but He uses human instruments through which to heal.

Let us look at a number of places in the New Testament that specifically state believers have gifts.

First Corinthians 12:7 says, *"But the manifestation of the Spirit **is given to each one** for the profit of all"* (emphasis added). With the Greek language, the tenses of the verbs are often of vital importance. In this verse, the verb is the continuous present tense. "To one is *regularly* given by the Spirit a word of wisdom," and so on. A person who has these gifts regularly manifests them.

"**Having then gifts** *differing according to the grace that is given to us, let us use them*" (Romans 12:6, emphasis added).

"*Each one* **has his own gift** *from God, one in this manner and another in that*" (1 Corinthians 7:7, emphasis added).

"*Do all have gifts of healings? Do all speak with tongues? Do all interpret?*" (1 Corinthians 12:30). This is an important verse because it includes one of the gifts people are hesitant about saying they have. When Paul wrote, "*Do all have gifts of healings?*" he clearly meant not all do, but some do. Otherwise, it would have been a meaningless rhetorical question. Here is clear scriptural authority for believers to say, "I have gifts of healings [or the interpretation of tongues, and so on].

You are clearly in the will of God to desire to have gifts.

God gave them to me. It doesn't make me any better than I was before, but I have to say, as a matter of experience, it is regularly manifested through me."

"*Earnestly desire the best gifts*" (1 Corinthians 12:31). If we could not have gifts, there would be nothing to desire. It is clear you are in the will of God to desire to have gifts.

"*Do not neglect the gift* **that is in you**, *which was given to you by prophecy with the laying on of the hands of the eldership*" (1 Timothy 4:14, emphasis added), and "*I remind you to stir up the* *gift of God **which is in you** through the laying on of my hands"* (2 Timothy 1:6, emphasis added). Paul wrote to Timothy in such a way that it is absolutely clear he considered Timothy to have a certain gift. If the gift is in you, then you have it.

*"As each one **has received a gift**, minister it to one another, as good stewards of the manifold grace of God"* (1 Peter 4:10, emphasis added). Peter used language similar to Paul's. You cannot minister what you do not have. First you have to receive it. Peter assumed all Christians would have gifts, thus enabling us to minister to each other. Real poverty is having nothing to contribute. That's the tragic condition of probably 90 percent of churchgoing Christians who profess faith in Christ. They have not received what God has made available to them, so they cannot give it. But this is not the will of God. No believer in Jesus Christ needs to be without his own distinctive manifestation of the Holy Spirit. *"But the manifestation of the Spirit is given to each one for the profit of all....But one and the same Spirit works all these things, distributing to each one individually as He wills"* (1 Corinthians 12:7, 11).

While all believers are given distinct gifts, this does not limit the Holy Spirit from manifesting any gift through any person at any time He wants to, because all the gifts are resident in Him. For example, if you are in an emergency and somebody is dying in front of you, you do not have to stand there and say, "I don't have the gift of healing, so there is nothing I can do." If you are filled with the Holy Spirit, you potentially have everything in Him. There is nothing to prevent the Holy Spirit from manifesting the gift of healing through you at that moment. However, the Scripture would not justify your saying you have the gift of healing unless it is regularly manifested in your life. God can give any manifestation that is needed to any person, but this is not the same as having the gift. We would not say that Balaam's donkey had the gift of prophecy. Why? Because it happened on only one occasion.

Paul therefore began and ended his list of the gifts of the Spirit by reminding us that, as believers, each one of us is entitled to his own specific manifestation(s) of the Holy Spirit in his life. Paul does not suggest that God rations to us just one manifestation. But if we live in our spiritual inheritance, we are entitled to enjoy the manifestations of the Holy Spirit in our lives. Any believer who is living without these manifestations is living below the level of God's provision for his life.

HAVE THE GIFTS BEEN WITHDRAWN FROM THE CHURCH?

Some people tell us that the gifts were withdrawn from the church after the first century. Yet Paul said the church is to exercise the gifts while it waits for the return of the Lord Jesus.

> *I thank my God always concerning you for the grace of God which was given to you by Christ Jesus, that you were enriched in everything by Him in all utterance and all knowledge, even as the testimony of Christ was confirmed in you,* **so that you come short in no gift, eagerly waiting for the revelation of our Lord Jesus Christ, who will also confirm you to the end, that you may be blameless in the day of our Lord Jesus Christ.**
>
> (1 Corinthians 1:4–8, emphasis added)

The closer the return of the Lord, the more we need to manifest the gifts. There is not a Scripture in the Bible that suggests the supernatural gifts of God's grace will ever be withdrawn from the church of Jesus Christ. When the church, as the bride, goes to meet Jesus, the Bridegroom, she will be adorned with the gifts He sent to her.

The reason why some believers do not have these manifestations is that they have never taken the vital step out of the natural into the supernatural. I believe the first essential step is the baptism in the Holy Spirit, accompanied by the miraculous manifestation of speaking in other tongues. Once you have entered into the realm of the supernatural, it is the will of God that you should continue to function in that realm.

The gifts are equipment for normal Christian living.

Spiritual gifts are not something remote from a bygone age; neither are they reserved for a few spiritual giants or preachers and missionaries in foreign lands. The New Testament reveals the gifts as part of the spiritual equipment for normal Christian living for believers throughout all ages until Christ returns.

THE ULTIMATE PURPOSE OF SPIRITUAL GIFTS

Let's close this chapter by discussing the purpose of the gifts from God's point of view. We often make the mistake of viewing His purposes and provision only from the perspective of what they will do for us. For instance, you hear people saying about the baptism in the Holy Spirit, "You'll feel wonderful if you get the baptism." You will not feel wonderful *all* the time. Sometimes you may feel worse than you have ever felt before because you may become aware of problems, needs, and spiritual forces you were not previously aware of. Others may say, "It'll help you tremendously with your study of the Bible," which is true. Or they may tell you, "You'll have power to witness." This is also a wonderful result of the baptism. However, all these reasons for receiving the baptism in the Holy Spirit are directed toward what it will do for you. The great reason for having the baptism in the Holy Spirit is what it will do for the body of Christ.

"[In] *one Spirit we were all baptized into one body*" (1 Corinthians 12:13). Why? To make us effective members of the body of Christ. This will glorify God. The Westminster Catechism includes this statement: "What is the chief end of man?" It is "to glorify God, and to enjoy Him forever." Few of us grasp the fact that the supreme end of life is to glorify God. Somebody once said to me, "If you don't exist for the glory of God, you've got no right to exist." That's the truth. Everything was created for God's pleasure. Why are spiritual gifts important? It is because they bring glory to God.

The book of Ephesians contains some absolutely breathtaking phrases in regard to this.

> *The God and Father of our Lord Jesus Christ...*[has] *predestined us to adoption as sons by Jesus Christ to Himself, according to the good pleasure of His will, to the praise of the glory of His grace, by which He has made us accepted in the Beloved....That we who first trusted in Christ should be to the praise of His glory.*   (Ephesians 1:3, 5–6, 12)

What's the ultimate purpose of God in adopting us as His children? That we may be for *"the praise of the glory of His grace."* I like the way one version translates the end of verse six: *"...which has made us graciously favored in the beloved."* Grace is heaped on us. Grace is given to us when we don't deserve it, making us the object of God's special favor. We are the object of His favor more than anything else in the universe because of our relationship with Jesus Christ.

I also like the version we previously read, *"He has made us accepted in the Beloved,"* because about one in five people in America has a basic problem of feeling rejected. I have ministered to scores of people whose basic problem was that, because of some traumatic experience in life—usually a lack of love from parents—they have gone through life feeling unwanted.

Yet, we who are the least worthy, who were the farthest off, have been made the closest. All the riches of God's favor have been heaped upon us so that we should be to the praise of the glory of His grace throughout eternity. This is where the gifts have a part to play. Ephesians 3:10 says, *"To the intent that now the manifold wisdom of God might be made known by the church to the principalities and powers in the heavenly places."* The church of Jesus Christ is to be the revelation to the whole universe of God's wisdom. Our English translation says *"manifold wisdom,"* but the Greek word is even stronger, meaning "infinitely varied wisdom." Our exercise of the gifts is a significant way in which God fulfills His purpose of making known His infinitely varied wisdom by the church.

In the next chapter, we will see more of this beautiful and vital connection between God's grace and the gifts He bestows on us.

CHAPTER TWO

CHARISMA: GRACE Gifts

The Greek word for *"gifts"* and *"gift"* in 1 Corinthians 12 is *charisma*. The nine gifts listed there are not the only *charisma* gifts mentioned in the Scriptures. Wherever a certain word recurs in Scripture, as *charisma* does, it is like a chain. It tends to show you passages you should consider together to obtain a more complete picture of what God is trying to reveal. Having an understanding of the other kinds of grace gifts enables us to put the nine gifts in their proper perspective. For example, in the last chapter, we saw the relationship between the gifts of the Spirit and the ministry gifts.

The word *charisma* is derived from the basic Greek noun *charis*. *Charis* is normally translated as *grace*. Grace may be defined as "the unmerited favor of God toward the undeserving and the ill-deserving." Nothing in ourselves presents any reason for God's offer of love, mercy, and favor. It is His grace that causes Him to do it.

Let us look at several important facts about the nature of God's grace that also apply to the nature of His grace gifts.

THE NATURE AND WORKING OF GOD'S GRACE

Grace Is Free

First, grace is free; it cannot be earned. The gospel is a manifestation of the grace of God; it is His favor toward those who didn't deserve it, but rather deserved judgment and condemnation because of their sin and rebellion. Although God does faithfully reward those who do good, this is not grace. Grace is on an altogether different level than reward for work.

Many religious people think they have to do something to earn God's grace and—even worse—most of them think they *have* done something to earn it. They are wrong in both respects. We can never do anything to earn the grace of God. The hardest thing for a religious person to realize is he has no claim on the grace of God whatever. We cannot please God more than by being willing to accept His grace without trying to earn it or be good enough.

Grace Is Given through God's Sovereignty

Second, God's grace is His sovereign choice. He is absolutely entitled to do whatever He desires with it. He does not owe anyone an account or explanation of the workings of His grace. The Lord says, *"I will have mercy on whomever I will have mercy, and I will have compassion on whomever I will have compassion"* (Romans 9:15).

Grace Comes through Jesus Christ

Third, grace has only one channel; there is only one way it comes to the human race, and that is by Jesus Christ. In John 1:17, we read, *"The law was given through Moses, but grace and truth came through Jesus Christ."* God does not give grace to anyone in any situation or circumstance apart from His Son.

Grace Comes to the Humble

Fourth, grace is offered to only one kind of person: the one who is humble. Both James and Peter quoted Proverbs 3:34 in their epistles: *"God resists the proud, but gives grace to the humble"* (James 4:6; 1 Peter 5:5). Again, if we pridefully think we have earned God's grace, we cannot receive it. We must receive it on the basis of humbly acknowledging we have not earned it.

Grace Comes through Faith

There is only one means by which grace is appropriated— by which you can actually have it in your life and experience— and that is faith. Ephesians 2:8 says, *"By grace you have been saved through faith, and that not of yourselves; it is the gift of God."*

Even faith is given by God. You cannot boast of having faith because, until God gave it to you, you did not have it. God offers you His grace only through Jesus Christ; it is offered only to the humble and it is appropriated only by faith in Him.

Grace Is Administered by the Holy Spirit

There is only one administrator or dispenser of the grace of God—the Holy Spirit. In Hebrews 10:29, He is called the *"Spirit of grace."* The Spirit administers God's grace just as He administers everything we receive through Jesus Christ.

CHARISMA THROUGHOUT THE NEW TESTAMENT

With this understanding of the nature of grace, or *charis*, we are in a position to see how grace applies to the grace gifts or *charisma*. Adding *"ma"* to *charis* transforms it from a general, abstract noun to a definite, specific noun. *Charisma* is grace made effective. Therefore, a *charisma* is a specific form, operation, or manifestation of the grace of God; it is grace made available in a particular way.

There are various places in the New Testament where the word *charisma* is used. Let us look at those instances to get a better idea of the meaning of this word and its associations so we can apply it to the nine spiritual gifts.

Charisma in Romans

When the apostle Paul was writing to the Christians at Rome, whom he had not yet met in person, he said, *"I long to see you, that I may impart to you some spiritual gift [charisma]"*

A spiritual gift is a specific manifestation of God's grace.

(Romans 1:11). Paul did not specify what gift or gifts he had in mind. Yet his use of the word *"spiritual"* immediately lets us know he was referring to gifts of which the Holy Spirit was the administrator through Jesus Christ.

In the fifth chapter of Romans, the word *charisma* occurs twice. In these instances, it is translated *"free gift,"* which especially emphasizes its association with grace. Paul was contrasting what happened to the human race through the sin of Adam to what is offered to the human race through the righteousness of Jesus Christ.

> But the **free gift** [charisma] is not like the offense. For if by the one man's offense many died, much more the grace [charis] of God and the gift [dorea] by the grace [charis] of the one Man, Jesus Christ, abounded to many.
>
> (Romans 5:15, emphasis added)

In this verse, Paul directly lined up grace and gift: *"the grace of God"* and *"the gift by the grace of...Jesus Christ."* The Greek word for the second instance of *"gift"* in this verse is *dorea*, meaning "a gratuity." It has the connotation of something freely given.

Paul emphasized that the channel, which is only through Jesus Christ, *"abounded to many."*

> *And the gift [dorea] is not like that which came through the one who sinned. For the judgment which came from one offense resulted in condemnation, but the **free gift** [charisma—the free gift of Jesus Christ] which came from many offenses resulted in justification.*
> (Romans 5:16, emphasis added)

Although the word *charisma* is not actually used in verse 17, we recognize the specific gift Paul was speaking of.

> *For if by the one man's offense death reigned through the one, much more those who receive **abundance of grace** and of the **gift** [dorea] **of righteousness** will reign in life through the One, Jesus Christ.* (emphasis added)

The free gift Paul was writing about is righteousness. It is tremendously significant that the first specified grace gift mentioned in the New Testament is this gift of righteousness. It is the first manifestation of God's grace in the lives of those who come to Him through Jesus Christ. God cannot do anything for us until He has made us righteous. Righteousness is a grace gift, a free unmerited gift. You either receive it as a gift or you do not have it.

Next, we come to this well-known verse: *"For the wages of sin is death, but the gift [charisma] of God is eternal life in Christ Jesus our Lord"* (Romans 6:23). Again, Paul drew a deliberate contrast between wages and grace gifts—wages being the due reward for what we have done. If you work five days a week at a certain fixed salary, at the end of the week you have earned your wages. That's your due reward. Paul said the due reward for the sins we have all committed is death. If you want justice, you can have it, for God is just. But the alternative to justice is His grace—not what you have earned, not what you are good enough for, not what you have worked for, but the free, unmerited grace gift of God, which is eternal life in Jesus Christ our Lord.

In Romans 8:10, Paul gave the connection between life and righteousness. *"And if Christ is in you, the body is dead because of sin* [the old, Adamic nature has died], *but the Spirit is life because of righteousness."* This life comes in by the Holy Spirit because we are reckoned as righteous. God cannot give life to the unrighteous. Eternal life comes in on the basis of Christ's righteousness imputed to us through faith in Him.

A *charisma* is an unconditional gift from God to us.

Moving on to Romans 11:29, Paul said, *"For the gifts [charisma] and the calling of God are irrevocable."* When God has given a gift, He does not change His mind. Suppose I gave one of my adult daughters a new car. If it were truly a gift, I could not subsequently withdraw it if she did something I disapproved of. Otherwise, it would only be a conditional loan.

Likewise, when God gives you and me gifts, including the gifts of the Spirit, He does not take them away, even if we misuse them. We are accountable for what we do with them, but because they are gifts, they are not revoked. This is true not only of the gifts of God, but also the calling of God. I have known a number of people who had the calling of an evangelist. In many respects, their lives were altogether out of order.

They might even have been drunks or acted in immoral ways. Yet every time they would preach, sinners would be saved. You may ask, "How can people like that be used by God?" It is because God gave them the gift, and He never takes away what He has given. If at any time my receiving a gift is conditional on my being good enough to continue having it, then it is not a grace gift. We do not receive a gift by earning it, deserving it, or being good enough for it. And we keep it unless we ourselves deliberately let it go—which can happen. Yet God never withdraws it. Understanding that a *charisma* is an unconditional gift is vital to our receiving and exercising spiritual gifts.

Notice that Paul lined up the word *gift* with the word *grace*. In Romans 12:6–8, he wrote,

> *Having then gifts [charisma,* grace gifts] *differing according to the grace [charis] that is given to us, let us use them: if prophecy, let us prophesy in proportion to our faith; or ministry, let us use it in our ministering; he who teaches, in teaching; he who exhorts, in exhortation; he who gives, with liberality; he who leads, with diligence; he who shows mercy, with cheerfulness.*

Paul listed seven specific types of *charisma.* The first is prophecy. The second is ministry. The Greek word for ministry means "serving," primarily in the practical realm. It is related to the word from which the term *deacon* is derived. This is essentially a form of service in the material realm of life. Next he listed teaching, exhortation, giving, and leading. The Greek word for giving refers to sharing, but it means sharing from our material substance, or our finances. The Greek word for leading is *proistemi*, which means to "be set over" or "at the head of." (See also 1 Thessalonians 5:12; 1 Timothy 3:4–5, 12;

5:17.) In 1 Timothy 3, there is a direct parallel between a man ruling his family and a man ruling the church, for Paul said, *"A bishop ["overseer" NASB] then must be...one who rules [proistemi] his own house well, having his children in submission with all reverence (for if a man does not know how to rule [proistemi] his own house, how will he take care of the church of God?)."* The authority of a father in his family, therefore, is a pattern for the authority of a leader in the church.

Last, we have the gift of showing mercy. I love to emphasize that showing mercy is a specific *charisma*. Not all the charisma gifts are dramatic. Many people are looking only for the sensational. Millions of people in this world need someone to show them mercy. There are many lonely people who are longing for someone to extend kindness to them. We have received God's mercy, and we have an obligation to show His mercy. The early church regularly took upon itself the responsibility of caring for the poor. Most modern churches have a committee for everything except caring for the poor. This is a grace ministry that is greatly neglected. But these are all types of charisma that are to be ministered by believers in the church.

> You cannot earn grace gifts—you can only receive them.

Charisma in 1 and 2 Corinthians

The book of 1 Corinthians probably has the largest number of occurrences of the word *charisma*, though Romans comes very close. First, Paul said to the church of Corinth, *"You come short in no gift [charisma], eagerly waiting for the revelation of our*

Lord Jesus Christ" (1 Corinthians 1:7). To *"come short"* means to be lacking in.

Paul told this church, which had some very serious moral problems, in effect, "I'm so glad you're not lacking in any gift. Every *charisma* is manifested among you." Think about the many problems in this church at Corinth. For example, there was open immorality—a man had taken his father's wife. Yet, from Paul's words, we can see that the believers nevertheless all had grace gifts. Why? Again, they did not have them by deserving them. I have noticed that people who are not religious often have much more faith to appropriate the grace gifts of God when they hear about them because they are never troubled by trying to earn them; they know they cannot do that. In contrast, good, religious people often find it very hard to receive grace gifts because they still think in the back of their minds somewhere, *I've got to do something to earn this.*

Paul's ministry to the Corinthians reminds us that receiving a gift does not necessarily change a person's character. God wants to change our character so that we become like His Son Jesus Christ, but that is not the basis on which we receive the gifts. We do not receive gifts because we are good; we receive them by faith.

In 1 Corinthians 7:7–8, Paul wrote,

For I wish that all men were even as I myself. But each one has his own gift [charisma] from God, one in this manner and another in that. But I say to the unmarried and to the widows: It is good for them if they remain even as I am.

What particular gift or manifestation of God's grace was Paul referring to in his own life? It was celibacy, the ability to live unmarried. He said, in effect, "I wish everybody had this gift so they could serve the Lord full-time, but I realize not everybody does." Every person has his or her own particular manifestation of God's grace that enables him to do what God has called him to do. It is not good for a person who does not have this gift to try to live as if he did. But I want you to notice that Paul affirmed this as a grace gift.

In 1 Corinthians 12:4, Paul wrote, *"There are diversities of gifts [charisma], but the same Spirit."* As we noted earlier, there are many different gifts, but it is the Holy Spirit who dispenses all of them. Paul then listed nine specific grace gifts, which are the focus of this book.

> *For to one is given the word of wisdom through the Spirit, to another the word of knowledge through the same Spirit, to another faith by the same Spirit, to another gifts of healings by the same Spirit, to another the working of miracles, to another prophecy, to another discerning of spirits, to another different kinds of tongues, to another the interpretation of tongues.* (vv. 8–10)

A little later, Paul said, *"But earnestly desire the best gifts [charisma]"* (v. 31). People cannot desire gifts if they do not know what the gifts are. Paul assumed Christians would become acquainted with what God's gifts are, with what is available to them. Note that when he said to desire the best gifts, he was not encouraging pride. The grace gifts are given only to the humble. A desire to receive spiritual gifts, in itself, is not wrong.

To understand what Paul meant by the *"best gifts,"* we need go to verse twenty-eight, where he said, *"And God has appointed these in the church: first apostles, second prophets, third teachers, after that miracles, then gifts of healings, helps, administrations ["governments" KJV], varieties of tongues."* Paul specified eight specific functions or ministries in the church: apostles, prophets, teachers, miracles, gifts of healings, helps, administrations or governments, and varieties of tongues. In summing up his teaching, Paul said to desire the best. Then which gifts are the best?

I doubt Paul arranged these gifts in an order of merit. I do not believe you can make an absolute list and say this is the order of their importance. The best gifts are those that best fulfill the function for which they were given. Therefore, whichever gift fulfills your situation and circumstances at the time is the best gift.

Whichever gift fulfills your situation at the time is the best gift.

A completely different type of *charisma* is mentioned in the following passage. Paul was referring to a certain experience in his own missionary ministry.

> *Yes, we had the sentence of death in ourselves, that we should not trust in ourselves but in God who raises the dead, who delivered us from so great a death, and does deliver us; in whom we trust that He will still deliver us, you also helping together in prayer for us, that thanks may be given by many persons on our behalf for the gift [charisma] granted to us through many.* (2 Corinthians 1:9–11)

Paul was referring to miraculous deliverance from extreme danger, and he called it a gift; it was a manifestation of God's grace. Possibly, Paul was talking about the situation at Lystra when he was stoned and dragged out of the city by his enemies and left for dead, but then stood up and walked away as though nothing had happened. (See Acts 14:8–20.) That supernatural intervention of God was a grace gift, and it came in answer to the prayers of many. It is important to understand that a sudden, dramatic, supernatural intervention of God, contrary to all we could normally expect, is a gift given by God's grace to meet the needs of a particular situation.

The context of Paul's remarks would seem to indicate that miraculous intervention normally comes in response to the prayers of a group rather than as a manifestation in the life of a particular individual. As Paul wrote, *"You also helping together in prayer for us, that thanks may be given by many persons on our behalf for the gift granted to us through many"* (2 Corinthians 1:11).

Another obvious example of divine, miraculous intervention in answer to the prayers of a group is when Peter was brought out of prison the night before he was to be executed, which is recorded in Acts 12. Clearly, this intervention of God must fall in the same category as a gift because it was not earned. It was the sovereign grace of God reaching down at a critical moment to spare Peter's life. If we consider grace gifts in this light, many of us may be able to look back on a supernatural, miraculous intervention in answer to prayer that meets the requirements of a *charisma*.

Charisma in 1 and 2 Timothy

In 1 Timothy 4:14, Paul gave words of advice to Timothy, whom he earlier called his *"son in the faith"* (1 Timothy 1:2): *"Do not neglect the gift [charisma] that is in you, which was given to you by prophecy with the laying on of the hands of the eldership."* In 2 Timothy 1:6, a very similar exhortation was given: *"I remind you to stir up the gift [charisma] of God which is in you through the laying on of my hands."* Timothy was apparently rather liable to allow timidity to keep him from exercising the gift God had given him. Paul therefore found it necessary in each of these epistles to exhort him, in effect, "Do not let that gift lie dormant; do not be content just to minister as if you did not have this particular gift. Stir it up; use it. It was given to you by God for His glory and to fulfill His purposes, and you are accountable for what you do with it." Likewise, we are accountable for what we do with the grace gifts of God in our lives.

Charisma in 1 Peter

The final instance of *charisma* in the New Testament is in 1 Peter 4:10: *"As each one has received a gift [charisma], minister it to one another, as good stewards of the manifold grace of God."* Peter did not expect any Christian to be lacking in grace gifts. He indicated every believer would receive gifts, and, on the basis of what they had received, they would be able to minister to others.

If Christians are going to minister, therefore, they must first receive. Large sections of the contemporary church seem to have nothing to give. The preacher can preach at them and exhort them to do this and that, but if they have nothing to do it with, how can they do it? One of the basic problems of the Christian church today is that we are operating in the natural. We trust in education, background, social environment, and so forth, rather than in God's grace and power. If we would let God give us grace gifts—which we do not have to earn or qualify for with education, training, or seminary background—we would be in a position to minister to others.

THE *Gifts* OF THE SPIRIT

THE VARIETY AND ABUNDANCE OF GOD'S GRACE

There are a total of twenty-six types of *charisma* or grace gifts mentioned in the New Testament, not counting those that repeat. We have looked at a number of them. Many are directly referred to in the Scriptures, while others are inferred.

1. righteousness (see Romans 5:15–17)
2. eternal life (Romans 6:23)
3. prophecy (Romans 12:6; 1 Corinthians 12:10)
4. ministry [serving] (Romans 12:7)
5. teaching (Romans 12:7)
6. exhortation (Romans 12:8)
7. giving (Romans 12:8)
8. leading (Romans 12:8)
9. showing mercy (Romans 12:8)
10. celibacy (see 1 Corinthians 7:7)
11. a word of wisdom (1 Corinthians 12:8)
12. a word of knowledge (1 Corinthians 12:8)
13. faith (1 Corinthians 12:9)
14. gifts of healings (1 Corinthians 12:9)
15. workings of miracles (1 Corinthians 12:10)
16. discernings of spirits (1 Corinthians 12:10)
17. different kinds of tongues (1 Corinthians 12:10)
18. the interpretation of tongues (1 Corinthians 12:10)
19. apostle (1 Corinthians 12:28)
20. prophet (1 Corinthians 12:28)
21. teacher (1 Corinthians 12:28)

22. helps (1 Corinthians 12:28)

23. administrations [governments KJV] (1 Corinthians 12:28)

24. evangelists (Ephesians 4:11)

25. pastors (Ephesians 4:11)

26. miraculous intervention (2 Corinthians 1:11)

Throughout this book, as we take an in-depth look at the nine spiritual gifts, the word I want you always to keep in mind is *grace*—the riches of God's grace, the abundance of God's grace, the variety of God's grace. I went into some detail in this chapter about the frequent use of *charisma* in the New Testament in order to stir you up to believe that God has an abundance for you, too. God never made two snowflakes or sets of fingerprints the same. Similarly, no two Christians are identical because God has enough grace, gifts, variety, and abundance for all of us. If you are living on limited rations of grace, God is not rationing you—you are rationing yourself! Open your heart and life to receive His plentiful gifts of grace.

Chapter 3

The Manifestation of the Spirit

Since there are twenty-six distinct facets or types of *charisma* in the Scriptures (see the complete list on pages 38–39), the natural question is, "Why are the nine gifts mentioned in 1 Corinthians 12:8–10 in a special category of their own?" To use scientific terms, we can think about the *charisma* as a "genus" (a class or category) and these nine gifts as one "species" in that genus. This leads to a second question, "What is the distinguishing feature of these gifts?"

The answer may be found in the verse that introduces the list: *"But the manifestation of the Spirit is given to each one for the profit of all"* (1 Corinthians 12:7). Obviously, these gifts are for a useful, practical, profitable purpose. Someone has said, "The gifts of the Holy Spirit are not toys, they're tools." Yet I believe the key word that distinguishes these nine from all other grace gifts is *"manifestation."* Manifestation refers to an open revelation to the senses, such as the eye or the ear.

The physical body of the believer in Jesus Christ is a temple in which the person of the Holy Spirit dwells. The apostle Paul said, *"Do you not know that your body is the temple of the Holy Spirit who is in you?"* (1 Corinthians 6:19). Yet the Holy Spirit within that temple is invisible; His presence cannot be perceived by any of the five senses. These nine distinctive manifestations of the Spirit are therefore evidence of the invisible Spirit dwelling in a believer. They are ways in which the invisible Holy Spirit is made manifest in that believer. Every one of these gifts is perceptible by the senses in some way or another.

Jesus taught Nicodemus about the Holy Spirit in terms of the wind: *"The wind blows where it wishes, and you hear the sound of it, but cannot tell where it comes from and where it goes. So is everyone who is born of the Spirit"* (John 3:8). None of us has ever seen the wind; its nature is to be invisible. Yet we know when the wind is blowing because we see the things the wind does: leaves come off trees, the trees all bend in a particular direction, the clouds go scurrying across the sky, dust swirls in the streets, and so on. These are *manifestations* of the wind. Similarly, no one sees the Holy Spirit indwelling a believer, but the things the Holy Spirit does from within that believer are manifestations of His presence. They are a distinctive revelation that He is there and operating in specific ways.

Spiritual gifts are for useful, practical, profitable purposes.

Some Christians have the idea that the Holy Spirit is so sacred, invisible, and spiritual that you can never get close to Him or feel or experience Him. This is not correct. It is important to understand it is scriptural to speak about manifestations of the Holy Spirit. The Holy Spirit has done much that was perceptible to people. I would like to illustrate this fact from two passages in the New Testament.

Acts 2 describes the events on the day of Pentecost, when the Holy Spirit descended from heaven to take up His dwelling within the members of the newly formed church of Jesus Christ on earth. There were clearly manifestations of the Holy Spirit on that day.

> *When the Day of Pentecost had fully come, they were all with one accord in one place. And suddenly there came a sound from heaven, as of a rushing mighty wind, and it filled the whole house where they were sitting. Then there appeared to them divided tongues, as of fire, and one sat upon each of them. And they were all filled with the Holy Spirit and began to speak with other tongues, as the Spirit gave them utterance.* (Acts 2:1–4)

The believers were filled with the Holy Spirit and began to speak in other languages—new languages they had not learned. It was these manifestations of the Spirit that drew the great crowd of people to hear the sermon Peter subsequently preached (see verses 14–40), which brought three thousand people to the point of faith in Jesus Christ (see verse 41). If there had not been any manifestations, no one beyond the disciples would have recognized the Holy Spirit had come. The Holy Spirit is known through His manifestations.

When Peter was coming to the climax of his message—after he had preached about Jesus, the course of His ministry, His death, His resurrection, and His ascension into heaven—he said,

> *This Jesus God has raised up, of which we are all witnesses. Therefore being exalted to the right hand of God, and having received from the Father the promise of the Holy Spirit, He poured out **this which you now see and hear.*** (Acts 2:32–33, emphasis added)

The people did not see and hear the Holy Spirit Himself, but they saw and heard what He did in and through the believers whom He had come to indwell. It is interesting to note the word *"this"* in verse thirty-three: *"this which you now see and hear."* The word is actually used several times in Acts 2. First, we read,

> When **this** sound occurred, the multitude came together, and were confused, because everyone heard them speak in his own language. Then they were all amazed and marveled, saying to one another, "Look, are not all these who speak Galileans? And how is it that we hear, each in our own language in which we were born?"
>
> (vv. 6–8, emphasis added)

It was the sound that attracted the crowd. Sound is a manifestation; it can be recognized through the sense of hearing. The verse is specific as to what astonished the multitude. They heard these Galilean fishermen speaking languages they recognized but knew the Galileans didn't know, languages they had never learned by natural understanding or education. This is the point at issue.

Continuing on, we read, *"So they were all amazed and perplexed, saying to one another, 'Whatever could **this** mean?'"* (v. 12, emphasis added). What does *"this"* refer to? It refers to the disciples speaking in languages they didn't know. Some of the people responded by saying, in effect, "These men are drunk. What are you listening to them for?" (See verse 13.)

Peter stood up and put them straight:

> Men of Judea and all who dwell in Jerusalem, let this be known to you, and heed my words. For these are not drunk,

as you suppose, since it is only the third hour of the day [No one gets drunk at nine o'clock in the morning]. *But* **this** *is what was spoken by the prophet Joel....*

(Acts 2:14–16, emphasis added)

"This" refers to the same thing, the speaking in other languages. What did Peter say about this speaking in other languages? *"This is what was spoken by the prophet Joel: 'And it shall come to pass in the last days, says God, that I will pour out of My Spirit on all flesh'"* (vv. 16–17). He was speaking of the promised outpouring of the Holy Spirit, predicted through the prophet. Peter again used the word *"this"* at the end of his declaration: "[Jesus] *being exalted to the right hand of God, and having received from the Father the promise of the Holy Spirit, He poured out* **this** *which you now see and hear"* (v. 33, emphasis added).

This incident of the first outpouring of the Holy Spirit shows that when the Holy Spirit comes to indwell the believer, He will produce manifestations out of that believer that can be seen and heard, that are perceptible by the senses. This is actually the evidence of His having come. Note what Paul said about his own preaching and ministry in 1 Corinthians:

And I, brethren, when I came to you, did not come with excellence of speech or of wisdom declaring to you the testimony of God. For I determined not to know anything among you except Jesus Christ and Him crucified. I was with you in weakness, in fear, and in much trembling. And my speech and my preaching were not with persuasive words of human wisdom, but in demonstration of the Spirit and of power, that your faith should not be in the wisdom of men but in the power of God. (1 Corinthians 2:1–5)

Many people imagine Paul was a great preacher, but this idea is contradicted by Scripture. He said, *"My speech and my preaching were not with persuasive words of human wisdom."* In 2 Corinthians 10:10, he quoted his enemies as saying his bodily presence was weak and his speech contemptible. I think Peter was a tremendous preacher, but Paul was not a "pulpit personality" at all. He wasn't a tremendous orator. How did he produce his results?

It wasn't by the education he received at the feet of the highly regarded Jewish teacher Gamaliel. (See Acts 5:34; 22:3.) Paul said, *"I...did not come with excellence of speech or of wisdom declaring to you the testimony of God. For I determined not to know anything among you except Jesus Christ and Him crucified"* (1 Corinthians 2:1–2). It wasn't uncommon boldness. He told the Corinthians, *"I was with you in weakness, in fear, and in much trembling"* (v. 3). In Acts 18:1–11, we read that Paul's life was in danger

Every believer should have personal experience of God's power.

when he was in Corinth, and he was afraid. But the Lord spoke to him in a vision and said, *"Do not be afraid, but speak, and do not keep silent; for I am with you, and no one will attack you to hurt you; for I have many people in this city"* (vv. 9–10).

So how did Paul produce his results? His preaching was *"in demonstration of the Spirit and of power"* (1 Corinthians 2:4). The word *"demonstration"* exactly corresponds with the word *manifestation* we have been looking at. The secret of Paul's ministry was not oratory, education, or even courage but the manifestation of the supernatural power of God—the demonstration of the working of the Holy Spirit in his life.

Likewise, believers are to demonstrate the power of the Holy Spirit through the supernatural gifts Paul enumerated in the twelfth chapter of 1 Corinthians. Paul said the purpose for this demonstration or manifestation is *that your faith should not be in the wisdom of men but in the power of God*" (1 Corinthians 2:5). The faith of every true Christian should not be based on intellectual or philosophical arguments, or on seminary training and degrees, though they can have their place, but on the personal experience of God's power.

When I was a missionary in East Africa, I came to a kind of crisis in ministering to the African students whom I was training to be teachers. They said yes to everything I said, but I never knew how much they really believed; the problem was too much acquiescence. One day I stood in front of the students in an assembly and said, "I want to thank you that you're so cooperative and obedient and willing to do what we ask. I know the reason why. Your education depends on us and you want education; it is your god." Then I said, "In the minds of most of you, there still remains a great big question mark." When I said that, they began to look at me. "The question in your minds is this: Is the Bible a book for Africans that you can read and trust, or is it just a white man's book that somebody has brought from another country, which doesn't really relate to Africans? Many of your own African elders are telling you it is just a white man's book that you better not spend your time trying to obey or to follow."

When I said that, there was quite a silence because I had said the very thing they were thinking. I added, "I want to tell you one more thing. I cannot answer that question for you." That statement surprised them because they thought missionaries could answer all questions. "There's only one way you'll find the answer to that question, and that is if you have a personal experience with the supernatural power of God in your life. When you have that experience, you'll know it didn't come from Britain, and it didn't come from America; it came from God."

I didn't argue with them. I dismissed the assembly, and I went away and prayed on this basis: "Lord, You said whatsoever a man sows, that shall he also reap. I've been sowing the Word of God to these young people, and You said if we sow to the Spirit we shall of the Spirit reap everlasting life. I'm holding You to Your Word." (See 2 Corinthians 9:6; Galatians 6:7–8.)

As time went on, I continued to preach the Word to the students, and I prayed. I did not do anything to coerce them into any type of acquiescence to the Christian faith. About six months later, there was a sovereign intervention of God in that college. It was quite remarkable. During the half-term break, most of the students went home for a long weekend. But

When we started to pray, the move of the Spirit began like a thunderclap.

there were about six or eight students whose homes were so far away they couldn't get there and back in time, so they stayed at the college. My wife and I thought we ought to do something for these lonely young men, so we invited them up to our home to have a cup of tea, which was a little unconventional in that setting in Africa.

They were not accustomed to a European or American style of living and socializing—sitting around on chairs and making conversation; they had never experienced that. So, we all sat there rather stiffly, and we served them tea, and they all took about five spoonfuls of sugar in each cup because they didn't often have it. Then I thought, *What are we going to do with them now?* I said maybe we should have a word of prayer. They obediently knelt down to pray, and when we started to pray something happened. It was like a thunderclap. Something came into that room and just hit us. Every one of those students started to pray out loud simultaneously. They were praying in a language I did not know, but I do not think it was other tongues; I think it was their own tribal language. Even though we were in a Pentecostal mission, the other missionaries later complained we made too much noise! But it was a divine act. I did not have anything to do with it. I could not have done it if I had stood on my head. God had intervened.

That event started something that went on for approximately four years. We had a sovereign, supernatural move of the Holy Spirit in that college. About three months later, I was speaking to the same group of students again, and I read them Acts 2:17, part of which we previously read: *"And it shall come to pass in the last days, says God, that I will pour out of My Spirit on all flesh; your sons and your daughters shall prophesy, your young men shall see visions, your old men shall dream dreams."*

I read this verse carefully and slowly and made sure they understood its meaning. Then I said, "I call you all to record that every single statement that is made in that verse has happened to you. It has not happened to somebody in another country or another college or another church. It has happened to you; you've experienced it. Your eyes have seen it, and your ears have heard it. This is God's testimony to you that you are living in the last days. Now, I am not asking you to believe something that a white man said or something that is in a white man's book. You have firsthand experiential evidence that this is true."

That did for them what no series of sermons, arguments, theological evidences, or seminary training could ever have done. It changed their entire attitude and behavior, and it made that college a place that was worth living in. It wasn't an effort to get them to pray. In fact, we had to stop them from praying because they wouldn't go to bed! They would pray all night in their dormitories. This was a sovereign intervention of God, and it came through the manifestation of the Holy Spirit. When they really found this was true in their own experience, we did not have to keep priming them and prodding them and pushing them along.

This is what the apostle Paul was saying. It is not enough to have sound doctrine, theology, education, arguments, and reasoning. True faith must not be based on the wisdom of men but on the power of God. In these last days, with the power of wickedness mounting on every hand and every type of assault against the faith of God and Jesus Christ and against His true church, no one is going to make it who doesn't have a personal experience of God's supernatural power in his or her own life. This is not a luxury—it is a necessity. The apostle Paul treated it that way: *"My speech and my preaching were not with persuasive words of human wisdom, but in demonstration of the Spirit and of power, that your faith should not be in the wisdom of men but in the power of God"* (1 Corinthians 2:4–5).

PART 2

Gifts OF REVELATION

CHAPTER 4

A WORD OF Wisdom

Let us now begin our in-depth look at the individual gifts of the Spirit with the gifts of revelation, starting with a word of wisdom.

COMPARING WISDOM AND KNOWLEDGE

It is worthwhile to note the similarities and differences between a word of wisdom and a word of knowledge. First, wisdom and knowledge cannot be separated into completely distinct categories because they are closely related. In fact, in our examination of all nine gifts of the Spirit, we are not seeking to draw hard-and-fast lines between them. They are like the colors of the rainbow: violet, indigo, blue, green, yellow, orange, red. It is easy to discern the different colors in a rainbow, but there is not one single point where you can say, for example, violet ends and indigo begins or indigo ends and blue begins. They blend into one another.

The same is true about spiritual gifts and other spiritual matters we are discussing. It is perfectly legitimate to speak separately about wisdom and knowledge, but there are also points where they meet; you cannot always say where wisdom ends and knowledge begins. There are times when you might wonder, "Was that a word of wisdom or a word of knowledge?"

Very frequently, where there is one, the other also comes into play.

Yet, generally, the difference between wisdom and knowledge is this: *knowledge gives us facts and wisdom shows us what to do about those facts.* If you have all the wisdom in the world but have no facts, you cannot make much direct application with it. On the other hand, even if you know all the facts, unless you have wisdom, you are likely to do the wrong thing with them.

This truth is beautifully summed up in a statement by King Solomon: *"The tongue of the wise uses knowledge rightly, but the mouth of fools pours forth foolishness"* (Proverbs 15:2). A wise person uses knowledge rightly. Many people have knowledge, but they don't use it correctly. I can think of one or two people who know many things but always seem to say them at the wrong time. Usually, they are trying to impress people with how much they know, but their timing and way of presenting it is out of place. They have knowledge, but they don't have wisdom regarding how to use it.

GOD'S WISDOM VERSUS THE WORLD'S WISDOM

We must also recognize that a spiritual word of wisdom is not the same as the world's wisdom. When I was a professional philosopher, I thought I was dealing in wisdom, yet this "wisdom" was intensely confusing. The more I confused people, the cleverer they thought I was—and probably the cleverer I thought I was, too. If you want concentrated confusion, just go to philosophy because that is where you will find it.

Yet, when I received the Lord Jesus Christ and dedicated my life to teaching and preaching the Word of God, I discovered God's wisdom is very different from what I was used to. His wisdom is very practical and to the point. It is not remote;

it is down-to-earth, and it is stated in simple terms. In fact, it is fascinating to study the teachings of Jesus in this regard. In the King James Version, in all of Jesus' recorded teachings, only once do you find a word that has more than four syllables. That word is *regeneration*. Much of His teaching is in words of one syllable, in which He speaks about lamps, oil, light, sheep, fish, life, death, love, hate. It is quite remarkable, and almost all historians would concur that no one ever spoke like this Man Jesus. His was a totally different kind of wisdom.

God's wisdom is not remote but very practical and to the point.

The Bible calls Solomon the wisest man who ever lived, and he summed up the nature of wisdom in Ecclesiastes 10:10: *"If the ax is dull, and one does not sharpen the edge, then he must use more strength; but wisdom brings success* [*"is profitable to direct"* KJV]." Wisdom is profitable or useful to direct, and it brings success. Wisdom is therefore directive, while knowledge is informative.

This verse always reminds me of when I tried to cut down a tree when I was a young boy living in southwest India with my parents. Every now and then, I would get a spurt of enthusiasm and ask my father if there was anything I could do to clean up the garden. One day he said, "There's a tree down there on the bank of the little stream that needs cutting down."

I went off and got the ax and started to hew away at this tree. After I had expended about thirty minutes of energy, the tree still stood defiant. All I had done was get very sweaty and develop blisters on my hands. The gardener came along, and he looked at me with a sort of smile of pity. He took the ax and sharpened it. Then he cocked his eye at the tree, looked at the point, and gave it about four blows with the ax, and it came down. I have always remembered that experience because I had made two mistakes. First, I had been using a blunt ax. Second, I had not been hitting the tree in the right place. The gardener, however, used the knowledge and wisdom he had gained to cut down the tree.

When I became a preacher, I came to see that, many times, I was guilty of the same thing in my preaching. Sometimes preachers use blunt axes. At other times, even when they have a sharp ax, they do not hit the tree in the right place. I remember an occasion when I preached in an Assemblies of God church in the United States and had a week of rather successful meetings. I was invited to preach in a Pentecostal church in Canada, and I am ashamed to admit I thought the same series of messages would do. I basically went through the series, with some changes, and plowed away. There were no results. Nothing. The last day, I discovered that, some years previously, there had been a tremendous rift in that church. They'd had a dispute about something, and the people who sat on the right-hand side of the church never spoke to the people who sat on the left-hand side—whether they were in church or not. They wouldn't talk to one another even if they met on the street. The prophet Elijah could have come from heaven and preached to them, and nothing would have happened until they were reconciled to one another.

If I had waited on God and been guided by the wisdom of the Holy Spirit, I am sure He would have given me the right message. But all I did was stand there and hew away for a week with a blunt ax, never cutting the tree down but getting a lot of blisters. I learned the hard way.

We must remember to sharpen the ax and let the Lord show us where to direct our blows. Many times, when I am led by the Holy Spirit, I will say something, and then I will ask myself, "What did I say that for?" But sure enough, it got the tree down. People have often come up to me afterward almost indignant or disturbed, asking, "Do you remember saying that?" I reply, "No, I don't remember saying it. I didn't intend to say it." They reply, "Well, that is what spoke to me." The Holy Spirit had given it to me as a word of wisdom.

A WORD OF WISDOM VERSUS EVERYDAY WISDOM

In addition, we must also realize a word of wisdom is not the same as everyday wisdom that God provides for us. There is a very precious promise in James 1:5: *"If any of you lacks wisdom, let him ask of God, who gives to all liberally and without reproach, and it will be given to him."* If you lack wisdom in your daily life for legitimate tasks and responsibilities, you can ask and be assured it will be given to you. The Bible does not have one good word to say about foolishness. God does not want us to be foolish, and He does not want us to be fooled, either.

A word of wisdom is a tiny portion of God's total wisdom given directly to us.

If you are having difficulty in your job, or if you are facing a particular life situation where your own wisdom is not sufficient, then you are entitled to go to God and ask Him for practical, everyday wisdom. It will help you to do a better job or to handle the situation better than you would have without it. This wisdom will not normally come in the form of a word of wisdom, however. It will come by a gradual illumination of your mind in which you understand what you should do.

A WORD OF WISDOM DEFINED

Then what is the gift of a word of wisdom? It is a tiny portion of God's total wisdom directly and supernaturally imparted by the Holy Spirit. *"For to one is given* [a] *word of wisdom through the Spirit"* (1 Corinthians 12:8).

God has all wisdom. But, fortunately for you and me, He does not give it to us all at once because it would completely submerge us. This gift is given by supernatural means because the results would not be available by natural means. It is imparted by the Holy Spirit in a way we could not get for ourselves.

MANIFESTATIONS OF A WORD OF WISDOM IN SCRIPTURE

Let us review some specific examples from the New Testament where this gift of wisdom was in operation, beginning with the ministry of Jesus and then moving on to examples from the early church. We will look at the way the gift was used and the kind of results it produced. In Jesus, we find the five ministry gifts perfectly demonstrated. He was the perfect apostle, prophet, evangelist, shepherd, and teacher. As He operated in these ministries, the various supernatural gifts of the Holy Spirit were also demonstrated to their perfection in Him.

Words of Wisdom about Fish and Men

The first example is from Luke:

When [Jesus] had stopped speaking, He said to Simon, "Launch out into the deep and let down your nets for a catch." But Simon answered and said to Him, "Master, we have toiled all night and caught nothing; nevertheless at Your word I will let down the net." And when they had done this, they caught a great number of fish, and their net was breaking. So they signaled to their partners in the other boat to come and help them. And they came and filled both the boats, so that they began to sink. When Simon Peter saw it, he fell down at Jesus' knees, saying, "Depart from me, for I am a sinful man, O Lord!" For he and all who were with him were astonished at the catch of fish which they had taken; and so also were James and John, the sons of Zebedee, who were partners with Simon. And Jesus said to Simon, "Do not be afraid. From now on you will catch men."

(Luke 5:4–10)

This incident is obviously supernatural. First, Jesus, who was trained as a carpenter, was able to tell an experienced fisherman where to put down his nets for a catch. Peter made his living at fishing, which is sufficient proof he was fairly good at it. He had fished all night at a certain place on the Lake of Gennesaret but had caught nothing. Jesus had come in the early morning and preached to the crowds on the shore. At the end of His message, He said, "Simon, launch out and let down your nets." Peter replied, "Lord, this isn't the time of day to fish. Besides, we have already fished here and there weren't any fish to catch." Yet notice what he added: *"Nevertheless at Your word I will let down the net."*

Jesus gave him a word of divine, directive wisdom regarding where to fish. When he followed that word, he caught so many fish the net broke; even with the help of his partners,

James and John, who also had a boat, they could not get all the fish into the boats, and their boats began to sink.

The effect this experience produced in Peter was tremendous spiritual conviction. He fell down at Jesus' knees and said, *"Depart from me, for I am a sinful man, O Lord!"* (Luke 5:8). Conviction is one of the results of the exercise of a true, supernatural word of wisdom. I have seen the gifts of a word of wisdom and a word of knowledge produce similar conviction. The sudden realization that God knows everything, that there is nothing hidden from Him, can break down the stubborn, proud heart of a sinner in a remarkable way.

Conviction is one result of a true word of wisdom.

This word of wisdom not only had a natural application—the catching of fish—but it also had a spiritual application. Immediately after Peter's declaration, Jesus told him, *"Do not be afraid. From now on you will catch men"* (v. 10). If they needed Jesus to give them directive wisdom as fishermen to catch fish, how much more would they need directive wisdom from Him when they began to preach to "catch" souls? In this incident, therefore, we see an important illustration of a word of wisdom. Peter received direction regarding how and where to fish, with a broader application of how and where Peter, James, and John would preach the gospel.

It was this demonstration of Jesus' supernatural wisdom that made these men willing to leave everything and follow Him. *"So when they had brought their boats to land, they forsook all and followed Him"* (v. 11). They must have felt that if this Man had the answers to that degree in the physical realm, it was safe to follow Him.

A Word of Wisdom about Transportation

The next illustration is from Matthew 21:1–7. The Scripture says that when Jesus and His disciples arrived at the summit of the Mount of Olives, near Jerusalem,

> *Jesus sent two disciples, saying to them, "Go into the village opposite you, and immediately you will find a donkey tied, and a colt with her. Loose them and bring them to Me. And if anyone says anything to you, you shall say, 'The Lord has need of them,' and immediately he will send them." All this was done that it might be fulfilled which was spoken by the prophet, saying: "Tell the daughter of Zion, 'Behold, your King is coming to you, lowly, and sitting on a donkey, a colt, the foal of a donkey.'" So the disciples went and did as Jesus commanded them. They brought the donkey and the colt, laid their clothes on them, and set Him on them.*

This was the beginning of Jesus' triumphal ride into Jerusalem, which we celebrate on Palm Sunday. It is important to see this was done in fulfillment of Old Testament prophecy, which is quoted in this passage. (See Zechariah 9:9.) Through the Scriptures, and by the Spirit of God, Jesus knew God's program for that day. He knew there was to be a donkey and a donkey's colt for Him to ride on. Then, by the revelation of the Holy Spirit, He knew where they could be found, so that He could direct His disciples there.

Most people would not allow you to take away their donkey and colt just because you said, "The Lord has need of them." Yet this was divine, directive wisdom, and God had prepared the owners' hearts to receive it. We see that the results of this word of wisdom were to open hearts and meet a practical need.

I want to emphasize this word of wisdom arose out of Jesus' knowledge of Scripture, and that a knowledge of Scripture is basic in revelation gifts.

A Word of Wisdom about Ministry

In our next example, a very urgent practical problem was solved by a word of wisdom. Acts 6 relates a dispute that threatened to divide the early church into Jewish Christians who spoke Aramaic or Hebrew (the "Hebrews"), and Jewish Christians who spoke Greek (the "Hellenists"):

> *Now in those days, when the number of the disciples was multiplying, there arose a complaint against the Hebrews by the Hellenists, because their widows were neglected in the daily distribution. Then the twelve summoned the multitude of the disciples and said, "It is not desirable that we should leave the word of God and serve tables. Therefore, brethren, seek out from among you seven men of good reputation, full of the Holy Spirit and wisdom, whom we may appoint over this business; but we will give ourselves continually to prayer and to the ministry of the word."* (Acts 6:1–4)

The first priority in spiritual matters is prayer and the ministry of the Word of God, to which the twelve apostles were called. Practical matters are important, but they are secondary, and it is not God's will that those who are called to the ministry of the Word and prayer should get sidetracked by having to supervise practical ministries. The Holy Spirit therefore gave the apostles a word of wisdom. They were to stay with their primary ministry, and the other believers were to nominate from among the congregation seven men whom the apostles could appoint to oversee the distribution of charitable gifts.

Acts 6:5 gives us the people's response to this word of wisdom: *"And the saying pleased the whole multitude."* This is another result of a word of wisdom. God's people immediately say, "That's it! That addresses the problem; this is what we have to do." Words of wisdom solve disputes, problems, and quandaries, and they bring unanimity.

Words of wisdom bring unanimity and solve problems.

The church chose seven men to oversee the distribution to the widows. *"Then the word of God spread, and the number of the disciples multiplied greatly in Jerusalem, and a great many of the priests were obedient to the faith"* (v. 7). This would not have happened if they had not solved the practical problem, because there would have been continuing division, frustration, and jealousy—and the moving of God's Spirit would have been hindered. We can see that, although this was a practical problem, it also had important spiritual ramifications, which were met by a word of wisdom.

Words of Wisdom about a Road and a Chariot

In Acts 8, we have an example from the ministry of the apostle Philip, who was later called Philip the evangelist. This example in the spiritual realm exactly parallels the incident in the physical realm in which Jesus told the disciples where to fish.

Now an angel of the Lord spoke to Philip, saying, "Arise and go toward the south along the road which goes down from Jerusalem to Gaza." This is desert. So he arose and went. And behold, a man of Ethiopia, a eunuch of great authority under Candace the queen of the Ethiopians, who had charge of all her treasury, and had come to Jerusalem to worship, was returning. And sitting in his chariot, he was reading Isaiah the prophet. Then the Spirit said to Philip, "Go near and overtake this chariot." So Philip ran to him, and heard him reading the prophet Isaiah, and said, "Do you understand what you are reading?" (Acts 8:26–30)

The background to this story is that Philip was in the midst of a tremendous move of God in the city of Samaria. Multitudes of people had been converted, and many miracles, wonders, and signs had taken place. Suddenly an angel came with a message, "Go down on the road that leads from Jerusalem to Gaza." This stretch of road was desert. There was no congregation and apparently no one to preach to in the desert. What was the purpose of going there? Yet Philip did not question it and was obedient. As he traveled this road, he came across a eunuch in a chariot. This eunuch was a top government official from the country of Ethiopia, and was also a devout Jewish convert. He had traveled to Jerusalem to worship and was reading the book of Isaiah out loud as he journeyed back to his home country.

The Holy Spirit told Philip to go up to the chariot. Philip was receiving divine direction. By this guidance, God placed Philip within earshot of the person He wanted him to reach. The whole thing had been prepared by God, and the man was just longing to know the answer to what he was reading in the fifty-third chapter of Isaiah, the great prophecy about the atonement of Jesus Christ. And Philip was able to explain to him the way of salvation.

This story about Philip reminds me of an incident that happened to a woman whom I know well. She was sitting in the Atlanta airport when she saw a young man whom we would perhaps categorize as a hippie. He was wearing bright purple clothes. She got the strongest urge to say to him what Philip said to the eunuch, "Do you understand what you're reading?" She fought this urge for quite a while and thought, *This is nonsense.* Eventually, she yielded to the Holy Spirit and said to the young man, "Do you understand what you're reading?"

A word of wisdom can open a person's heart to God.

He wasn't reading anything at that moment, but her question got them into conversation. He was from New England, and his parents were wealthy and respectable people, but he had become desperate to find the meaning of life, to find something that wasn't phony or superficial, and he had run away from home. He got in with a group of hippies and went through the various experiences they often go through. He decided he wasn't getting anywhere and left to live somewhere in the wilderness for a time with practically nothing but the barest essentials of life. He took nothing with him to read except the New Testament. While he was out there reading the New Testament, even though he sincerely desired to find the truth, he could not figure out what it was all about. Yet reading the New Testament had made such an impact on him that he decided he must go home and be reconciled to his parents. The only clean clothes he had were those purple ones, so there he was in the Atlanta airport in his purple attire waiting to catch a plane back to New England and still trying to find the meaning of life.

Because the woman had asked if he understood what he was reading, he eventually opened up and began to tell her all about his struggle to understand the New Testament. She was able to explain to him briefly the plan of salvation. It really was just like an incident from the book of Acts. The result of the word of wisdom was the same—the young man had an open heart. Out of all the people in the Atlanta airport, there was one person who needed to be approached at that moment. No one, in the natural, could have known who that was. But by this directive word of wisdom, the woman was led to talk with exactly the right person.

A Word of Wisdom about People God Wanted to Save

In Acts 10, we have another example that shows how much this gift of wisdom is used to direct the servants of the Lord concerning when and where to go in their ministries. A Roman centurion named Cornelius, who lived in the city of Caesarea and was a devout believer in God, had received a visitation from an angel, who told him to send men to Joppa for Simon Peter. While the men were on their way,

Peter went up on the housetop to pray, about the sixth hour. Then he became very hungry and wanted to eat; but while they made ready, he fell into a trance and saw heaven opened and an object like a great sheet bound at the four corners, descending to him and let down to the earth. In it were all kinds of four-footed animals of the earth, wild beasts, creeping things, and birds of the air. And a voice came to him, "Rise, Peter; kill and eat." But Peter said, "Not so, Lord! For I have never eaten anything common or unclean." And a voice spoke to him again the second time, "What God has cleansed you must not call common." This was done three times. And the object was taken up into heaven again.

(Acts 10:9–16)

Peter was being directed by God against his own natural will, inclination, background, and training to go to the house of a Gentile and bring him the message of the gospel. After arriving at Cornelius's house, he said, *"You know how unlawful it is for a Jewish man to keep company with or go to one of another nation. But God has shown me that I should not call any man common or unclean"* (v. 28).

This spiritual insight and Peter's agreeing to go with Cornelius's messengers were the result of the direction he received from God. While Peter spoke to Cornelius, along with his family and friends, the Holy Spirit fell on them, and they spoke in tongues and praised God. The result was a tremendous, new addition to the church of Jesus Christ. But the wisdom that paved the way for it was given through a supernatural word from God in the form of a vision Peter received during prayer.

A Word of Wisdom about Law versus Grace

In Acts 15, the whole church in Jerusalem came together to debate a very critical problem—what should be required of the Gentile converts who were beginning to flood into the church?

Certain men came down from Judea and taught the brethren, "Unless you are circumcised according to the custom of Moses, you cannot be saved." Therefore, when Paul and Barnabas had no small dissension and dispute with them, they determined that Paul and Barnabas and certain others of them should go up to Jerusalem, to the apostles and elders, about this question....And when they had come to Jerusalem, they were received by the church and the apostles and the elders; and they reported all things that God had done with them. But some of the sect of the Pharisees who believed rose up, saying, "It is necessary to circumcise them, and to command them to keep the law of Moses." Now the apostles and elders came together to consider this matter. And when there had been much dispute.... (Acts 15:1–2, 4–7)

Paul and Barnabas had been out on their first missionary journey and had seen wonderful results among the Gentiles. God had worked with them supernaturally, and there had been many miracles, healings, and conversions. Yet when they came back to Jerusalem with this report, some of the Jews who were believers in Jesus Christ but Pharisees by background said, in effect, "If these Gentiles want to become Christians, they have to come under the law of Moses and be circumcised." The decision as to how they were to treat Gentile converts

A word of wisdom goes hand in hand with a word of knowledge.

who were coming into the church involved fundamental questions of the nature of salvation through Jesus Christ.

They first heard Peter, who reminded them of what had happened when God supernaturally directed him to the home of Cornelius:

God, who knows the heart, acknowledged them by giving them the Holy Spirit, just as He did to us, and made no distinction between us and them, purifying their hearts by faith. (Acts 15:8–9)

Next, we read, *"Then all the multitude kept silent and listened to Barnabas and Paul declaring how many miracles and wonders God had worked through them among the Gentiles"* (v. 12). In other words, Paul and Barnabas were saying God had borne supernatural testimony to their ministry to the Gentiles, and you cannot resist what God is doing. This did not settle the question, however.

After [Paul and Barnabas] *had become silent, James answered, saying, "Men and brethren, listen to me: Simon* [Peter] *has declared how God at the first visited the Gentiles to take out of them a people for His name. And with this the words of the prophets agree, just as it is written: 'After this I will return and will rebuild the tabernacle of David, which has fallen down; I will rebuild its ruins, and I will set it up; so that the rest of mankind may seek the LORD, even all the Gentiles who are called by My name, says the LORD who does all these things.' Known to God from eternity are all His works."* (vv. 13–18)

James followed his comments with a directive word of wisdom, but let us notice first that he based that wisdom on his knowledge of Old Testament Scripture. (See Amos 9:11–12.) Again, a word of wisdom always goes hand in hand with a knowledge of the Word of God. Here is James's word of wisdom:

Therefore I judge that we should not trouble those from among the Gentiles who are turning to God, but that we

write to them to abstain from things polluted by idols, from sexual immorality, from things strangled, and from blood.
(Acts 15:19–20)

This word of wisdom included four simple requirements and brought complete unanimity to the assembled church.

Then it pleased the apostles and elders, with the whole church, to send chosen men of their own company to Antioch with Paul and Barnabas [with this message].   (v. 22)

The message was this:

For it seemed good to the Holy Spirit, and to us, to lay upon you no greater burden than these necessary things: that you abstain from things offered to idols, from blood, from things strangled, and from sexual immorality. If you keep your-selves from these, you will do well.   (vv. 28–29)

Note how remarkable this was. There must have been many thousands of Jewish believers gathered, since this meeting involved the whole church in Jerusalem. Consider the number of people present who were bitterly opposed on this matter. Neither side was going to give in. And yet, the divine, directive word of wisdom came in and settled it. These opposing sides came to *complete unanimity.* There was peace, calm, unity—and spiritual progress. The rest of the chapter says the gospel moved on victoriously. This is a clear example of how important a word of wisdom is.

A Word of Wisdom about Location

A final example of a word of wisdom directing ministry is during Paul's second missionary journey. He and Silas had gone into what is known today as Asia Minor. They had finished going through the area that Paul and Barnabas had covered in the first missionary journey, and they were wondering where to go on from there.

> *Now when they had gone through Phrygia and the region of Galatia, they were forbidden by the Holy Spirit to preach the word in Asia. After they had come to Mysia, they tried to go into Bithynia, but the Spirit did not permit them. So passing by Mysia, they came down to Troas. And a vision appeared to Paul in the night. A man of Macedonia stood and pleaded with him, saying, "Come over to Macedonia and help us." Now after he had seen the vision, immediately we sought to go to Macedonia, concluding that the Lord had called us to preach the gospel to them.* (Acts 16:6–10)

Words of wisdom can produce open doors and spiritual progress.

This is remarkable. The province of Asia, which is on the western coast of Asia Minor, was in the direction they were heading, but the Holy Spirit told them not to go there. Jesus had told His followers, *"Go into all the world and preach the gospel to every creature"* (Mark 16:15). And here they were, trying to go to the province of Asia, and the Holy Spirit said no.

Then they thought they would go north to the southern shore of the Black Sea, Bithynia, but the Holy Spirit said no. What were they to do? They moved northwest, and God showed them they were to go to Macedonia, where they saw a tremendous move of God.

They experienced this move of God because they were directed by Him to go there. The door was open, the hearts of the people were open, and the way was prepared for them. Notice they had to be sufficiently obedient to accept the answer of no twice, and it took quite a while to get to Troas. All that time, they were walking in faith. Then came the vision with the man pleading with them to come to Macedonia, which was in what is today the northern part of Greece. This marks the first time the gospel was brought from Asia Minor to Europe proper. This was one of the most critical transitions in the history of the church. Paul and Silas could never have had any idea how church history was going to unfold in the next nineteen centuries. Yet the one place where the gospel was preserved and from which it was ultimately sent forth again in missionary enterprise was Europe.

In summary, a word of wisdom is associated with a knowledge of Scripture, and when it is manifested in accordance with the will of God, it commonly produces these results: conviction, open hearts, unanimity, open doors, and spiritual progress.

TIMING IS ESSENTIAL

Let us note one final point about wisdom. Later on in Paul's second missionary journey, he did go to the city of Ephesus, which is the chief city of the province of Asia. There, he had possibly the greatest and most dramatic results of his entire ministry. Yet, previously, the Holy Spirit had said not to go there. We must realize that timing is essential. Paul was to go to Asia, but not at the time he originally wanted to. I have seen thousands of dollars wasted and precious lives frustrated on the mission field by people being in the right place at the wrong time. They lacked divine, directive wisdom. Solomon grasped the importance of timing and wrote these familiar words:

> *To everything there is a season, a time for every purpose*
> *under heaven: a time to be born, and a time to die; a time*
> *to plant, and a time to pluck what is planted; a time to kill,*
> *and a time to heal; a time to break down, and a time to build*
> *up.* (Ecclesiastes 3:1–3)

How do we answer the question, Do we break something down, or do we build something up? It depends on the time. Do we plant or do we harvest? It depends on the time. You cannot always say absolutely yes or absolutely no to a question concerning wisdom. The time factor is decisive. Who reveals the right time? The Holy Spirit. And one main way He does so is by the directive word of wisdom.

CHAPTER 5

A WORD OF *Knowledge*

A WORD OF KNOWLEDGE DEFINED

I n the last chapter, I defined a word of wisdom as a tiny portion of God's total wisdom imparted by the Holy Spirit. A word of knowledge has a parallel definition. It is a tiny portion of God's total knowledge supernaturally imparted by the Holy Spirit. *"To another* [a] *word of knowledge* [is given] *through the same Spirit"* (1 Corinthians 12:8).

Like a word of wisdom, supernatural knowledge does not come by natural reasoning, education, or training but directly by the Holy Spirit, and it is operated only under God's control. I cannot have a word of knowledge merely by the exercise of my will. I may need knowledge, and I may be open to receiving it from God, but whether He gives it is ultimately in His hands.

MANIFESTATIONS OF WORDS OF KNOWLEDGE IN SCRIPTURE

Let us look at some examples of words of knowledge in the New Testament. We will again begin with the ministry of Jesus Himself because, once more, Jesus is the perfect pattern.

WORDS OF KNOWLEDGE ABOUT CHARACTER AND LOCATION

The background to this first example is that Philip had invited Nathanael to meet Jesus, whom Philip said was the Messiah. When Nathanael learned Jesus came from Nazareth, he could scarcely believe anything as good as the prophesied Messiah could come from that town. Nathanael was therefore brought to Jesus in a very dubious, questioning, rather critical attitude of mind.

> *Jesus saw Nathanael coming toward Him, and said of him, "Behold, an Israelite indeed ["true Israelite" NIV], in whom is no deceit!"* (John 1:47)

Note that Jesus referred to him as a true Israelite. What quality made him a real Israelite? There was no deceit or guile in him. Most of us would agree that is a very unusual thing in a person. Let us consider why Jesus may have made this statement. The forefather of the Israelites was Israel, whose name was originally Jacob. Jacob means "supplanter" or "cheat." This was essentially Jacob's character. Yet after God had dealt with him for many years, he had an encounter with the Lord in which his name was changed to Israel, which means "he shall be a prince with God." The basis of that change was getting the crookedness out of Jacob. Therefore, anybody who is called an Israelite should have had the crookedness taken out of him. And Jesus said of Nathanael, "Here is a real Israelite. There's no deceit in him."

Nathanael's response was, in essence, "You have never met me before. How do You know what kind of a person I am?" *"Jesus answered and said to him, 'Before Philip called you, when you were under the fig tree, I saw you'"* (John 1:48). Jesus had not seen him by natural sight, but by a vision or revelation of the Holy Spirit. Perhaps Nathanael had been praying under the fig tree. To his amazement, what he thought was a private moment was known to Jesus. Note his reaction. *"Nathanael answered and said to Him, 'Rabbi, You are the Son of God! You are the King of Israel!'"* (v. 49). He experienced immediate, intense conviction. This result is similar to the result we saw with a word of wisdom.

I have observed the gift of a word of knowledge in operation many times, and I have noticed it normally produces this result. It is often manifested in healing services. When a preacher can tell a person the exact nature and location of his pain or sickness without any natural means of knowing, it immediately produces conviction. It also very often produces faith because

A word of knowledge reveals a tiny portion of God's total knowledge.

people realize if God knows what the problem is, then He can heal it. Many times, therefore, a word of knowledge is used as a tool to bring faith into operation for healing.

A Word of Knowledge about Personal History

A second illustration of a word of knowledge is the well-known story of Jesus' meeting with the Samaritan woman at the well. He began by asking her for a drink of water. She was surprised, they got into conversation, and He began to speak to her about living water that would not have to be drawn continuously from a well. Let us continue their conversation from that point.

The woman said to Him, "Sir, give me this water, that I may not thirst, nor come here to draw." Jesus said to her, "Go, call your husband, and come here." The woman answered and said, "I have no husband." Jesus said to her, "You have well said, 'I have no husband,' for you have had five husbands, and the one whom you now have is not your husband; in that you spoke truly." The woman said to Him, "Sir, I perceive that You are a prophet." (John 4:15–19)

The woman knew perfectly well there was no natural means by which Jesus could have known these details of her past. When He spoke them, her defenses were immediately broken down, and she said, "You're a prophet."

I had an experience related to this. I was preaching in a street meeting in London, England, and I was talking about the Samaritan woman and the living water that Jesus gives. I got to this point in the story, and I was gripped by the fact that if you want the living water, you have to put your life right. I spoke about how this woman wanted the living water, but she didn't want to deal with the fact that she was living with a man who was not her husband. I emphasized this point, and there was a young woman there who became so furious with me she almost assaulted me. Why? She had run away from her husband and was living with another man. Of course, I wasn't speaking about her life with the same clarity with which Jesus spoke to the woman at the well. Yet even coming as close as that immediately produced conviction in the woman.

A Word of Knowledge about Dishonesty

One person who definitely manifested the gift of a word of knowledge was the apostle Peter. It was very evident in his ministry. In Acts 5, we find a very startling incident in the early church in which his gift was manifested. The background of the situation was that, at this time in the life of the early church, believers were selling their land and other possessions and bringing the money to the apostles for the work of the church and the ministry.

> *But a certain man named Ananias, with Sapphira his wife, sold a possession. And he kept back part of the proceeds, his wife also being aware of it, and brought a certain part and laid it at the apostles' feet.* (Acts 5:1–2)

I want to point out their sin was not keeping back part of the price. It was pretending they had given the whole amount.

> *But Peter said, "Ananias, why has Satan filled your heart to lie to the Holy Spirit and keep back part of the price of the land for yourself? While it remained, was it not your own? And after it was sold, was it not in your own control? Why have you conceived this thing in your heart? You have not lied to men but to God." Then Ananias, hearing these words, fell down and breathed his last. So great fear came upon all those who heard these things. And the young men arose and wrapped him up, carried him out, and buried him. Now it was about three hours later when his wife came in, not knowing what had happened. And Peter answered her, "Tell me whether you sold the land for so much?" She said, "Yes, for so much." Then Peter said to her, "How is it that you have agreed together to test the Spirit of the Lord? Look, the feet of those who have buried your husband are at the door, and they will carry you out." Then immediately she fell down at his feet and breathed her last. And the young men came in and found her dead, and carrying her out, buried her by her husband. So great fear came upon all the church and upon all who heard these things.* (vv. 3–11)

If I had been there, great fear would have come upon me, I'll tell you. Think of the power! These two people just couldn't live in the presence of the supernatural knowledge of the Holy Spirit. How many people are trying to cheat God today by pretending to be better and to give more than they really do?

This was a cautionary judgment of God. It does not mean He deals with every hypocrite like this, but it shows what God thinks of hypocrites. His opinion does not change, though His method of dealing with hypocrisy is not always the same. This is really the only way the church can be kept pure. Some churches have a statement of fundamentals of what they believe, and they ask people to acknowledge their acceptance of it. Ananias and Sapphira would probably have said amen to every fundamental. Yet here was something they could not get around. They were lying, but the supernatural knowledge of almighty God revealed it. The Holy Spirit in Peter knew what Peter could not have known, and he said, in essence, "You haven't been lying to me. You've been lying to the Holy Spirit."

A word of knowledge can also include a word of wisdom.

We are dealing with a living God. The Bible says, *"All things are naked and open to the eyes of Him to whom we must give account"* (Hebrews 4:13). The problem with most church members is they do not realize they are dealing with God Himself. They think they are dealing with the church board, the deacons, or the pastor. You can fool any preacher some of the time. Yet there is one Person none of us ever fools, and that is God.

A Word of Knowledge about a Chosen Servant of God

In Acts 9, we find another example of a word of knowledge. Saul of Tarsus was on his way to Damascus to imprison and condemn those who believed in Jesus in that city. As Saul neared Damascus, the Lord Jesus stopped him on the road with a bright light, and then revealed Himself to him. Saul was struck blind, and he had to be led by the hand into the city.

A believer named Ananias lived in Damascus. He wasn't an apostle, and he wasn't an evangelist. The Bible just calls him a *"disciple"* (Acts 9:10). Some people do not believe God gives gifts and revelations to anybody except preachers, missionaries, and other Christian leaders. But here we see God gave a word of knowledge to this disciple Ananias.

> *Now there was a certain disciple at Damascus named Ananias; and to him the Lord said in a vision, "Ananias." And he said, "Here I am, Lord." So the Lord said to him, "Arise and go to the street called Straight, and inquire at the house of Judas for one called Saul of Tarsus, for behold, he is praying. And in a vision he has seen a man named Ananias coming in and putting his hand on him, so that he might receive his sight."* (vv. 10–12)

Ananias was given Saul's exact name and address, and he was able to know what Saul had seen in a vision. Note that the knowledge he received also included a directive word of wisdom: if Ananias went to Saul and laid his hands on him, he would receive his sight.

At first Ananias was unwilling to go. He protested to the Lord that this man had come to Damascus to persecute the Christians. But the Lord persuaded him. *"Go, for he is a chosen vessel of Mine to bear My name before Gentiles, kings, and the chil-dren of Israel"* (Acts 9:15). His obedience resulted in Saul's being brought into fullness of faith in Jesus Christ. It was a crucial moment in God's dealings with the early church. Because Ana-nias could go to Saul and say, with knowledge and wisdom, *"Brother Saul, the Lord Jesus, who appeared to you on the road as you came, has sent me"* (v. 17), Saul's heart was opened to the truth. Saul became the apostle Paul, evangelized much of the Gentile world, and wrote a large portion of the New Testament.

A Word of Knowledge for Confirmation

In the previous chapter, we looked at a passage in Acts 10 as an example of a word of wisdom. Peter was directed by a vision to preach to the Gentiles in Caesarea. Notice that this wisdom was followed by a word of knowledge. As I said, these two gifts often work together. After Peter had the vision, the men from the house of Cornelius in Caesarea arrived at the gate and were knocking. Peter was still on the rooftop, where he had been praying, pondering the vision. We read,

> *While Peter thought about the vision, the Spirit said to him, "Behold, three men are seeking you. Arise therefore, go down and go with them, doubting nothing; for I have sent them." Then Peter went down to the men who had been sent to him from Cornelius.* (Acts 10:19–21)

Before Peter knew through natural means that the men were there, or who had sent them, the Holy Spirit told him. This word of knowledge served as confirmation for the vision he had previously received. At this point, God had to put a great deal of pressure on Peter to get him to go and preach to Cor-nelius because it was contrary to his whole nature, background, and upbringing to go to the house of a Gentile, much less bring him the gospel. Therefore, a word of wisdom was followed by a word of knowledge, and the word of knowledge served as confirmation of the word of wisdom that had previously been given.

My wife Lydia told me about an incident that occurred in Jerusalem before she met me. There was rioting and war between the Arabs and Jews, and God revealed to her a situation of great danger. In a night vision, she saw blood on the bottom step of the stairs that led down from her front door. She was leading by the hand one of the little girls she was taking care of—who became our adopted daughter, Anna—and she lifted her over this pool of blood, where a man had been killed. When she saw this in the vision, she prayed, "Lord, I don't know what is going to happen. But if I'm going to be in that situation, be with me and protect us." About two days later, exactly what she had seen in the vision happened, and they were safe. Confirmation such as this lets a believer know God already knew about the situation, He was with them, and He took them through.

Words of knowledge can convict, confirm, and prepare.

A WORD OF KNOWLEDGE FOR PREPARATION

In Acts 20, while Paul was on his way to Jerusalem, he met with the elders of the Ephesian church. He told them various believers in the churches he had stopped to visit during his journey had received words of knowledge about him from the Holy Spirit. Paul said to them,

*And see, now I go bound in the spirit to Jerusalem, not
knowing the things that will happen to me there, except that
the Holy Spirit testifies in every city, saying that chains and
tribulations await me.* (Acts 20:22–23)

We do not know the details, but in *every city* where Paul
had met together with believers, the Holy Spirit had warned
him that *"chains and tribulations"* were awaiting him in Jerusalem.

I had a similar experience when I was preaching in Den-
mark after we had returned from East Africa. I had a certain
message I felt the Lord had given me, which was that the harvest hour was at hand and it was the time for the harvest. I
preached it in three or four different congregations over one
weekend. The remarkable thing was that, in every congregation, when I finished that message, it was followed immediately
by an utterance in an unknown tongue and the interpretation
in the Danish language bearing testimony by the Holy Spirit
to the truth of what I said. The people in those congregations
were quite different, and they did not have any direct contact
with one another. Yet in every congregation, the Holy Spirit,
through the gifts of the Spirit, bore testimony. I want you to
know these things still happen today.

As Paul continued his journey to Jerusalem, he reached
the city of Caesarea. This was almost the last stage of the journey. In Acts 21, we read that Paul received another revelation
through a prophet named Agabus.

*And as we stayed many days, a certain prophet named
Agabus came down from Judea. When he had come to us,
he took Paul's belt, bound his own hands and feet, and said,
"Thus says the Holy Spirit, 'So shall the Jews at Jerusalem*

bind the man who owns this belt, and deliver him into the hands of the Gentiles.'"   (Acts 21:10–11)

Here was yet another word of knowledge along the same lines. "Your own people are going to bind you and betray you into the hands of the Romans, the Gentiles." Notice how gracious the Holy Spirit is. If we are prisoners of God, we are prisoners of love. The Holy Spirit did not cause Agabus to bind Paul's hands and feet but to bind his own hands and feet. Paul had the option of whether he would step into that position or not. It was up to his free will.

I also want to point out something that perhaps you would not realize if you are not familiar with Jewish culture. The ultimate betrayal for a Jew is to betray a fellow Jew into the hands of Gentiles. That is absolutely the last and lowest act they would commit. And the ultimate betrayal was when Jesus was betrayed into the hands of the Romans.

When Lydia and I were in Jerusalem in 1947–48, there were Jewish terrorists at work, and they were brutal. They would shoot people down in the streets, refuse to let anybody help them, and watch them die. I am not taking sides about this, but, in many cases, respectable Jewish citizens knew who these people were but said nothing about it. They would never betray them into the hands of the British or any other Gentile. Unless you have this background, you cannot appreciate what it meant for Paul to hear that he would be betrayed by his own people to the Romans.

What was the result of Paul's being given this word of knowledge several times along his route to Jerusalem? It was the preparation of his own heart. There is a proverb that says, "Forewarned is forearmed." He was being given mental and spiritual preparation for the tremendous ordeal that lay ahead of him.

RESULTS OF A WORD OF KNOWLEDGE

Let us then summarize the results that are frequently produced by a word of knowledge. The most conspicuous result is that it brings conviction of the truth. Second, it confirms something God has perhaps been showing us by some other means. Third, in certain circumstances, it prepares us for what is to come.

CHAPTER 6

Discernings OF SPIRITS

❧❧❧

Discernings of spirits is the third in the category of the gifts of revelation. *"To another* [is given] *discerning*[s] *of spirits"* (1 Corinthians 12:10). Let us consider briefly the meaning of discernment.

DISCERNMENT DEFINED

The word *discern* may be defined as "to recognize and distinguish between." While knowledge is the impartation of a fact, discernment is a form of direct perception. The result may be the same, but the means is different.

Discernment can come in different ways. At times, it may come as a vision where you actually see something that is not there in the natural. Let us look at two very obvious examples of this in the Scriptures.

First, John the Baptist saw the Holy Spirit descending upon Jesus as a dove. Other people who were present apparently did not see this, but John was given spiritual discernment. (See John 1:32–34.) Second, in the book of Revelation, the apostle John was granted a vision of three unclean spirits like frogs coming out of the mouth of the dragon, the beast, and the false prophet. (See Revelation 16:13–14.) I have met many people who have seen evil spirits in the form of animals, such as foxes, mice, bats, snakes, and frogs. This is not to say the animal itself is the evil spirit, but this is how it is revealed. These are examples of people seeing clear visions of what is not there in the natural.

Yet I think discernment is not commonly given to believers through such visions. It usually comes in the form of a person seeing what is there in the natural, but seeing it with the understanding of the Holy Spirit.

This is how I experience the gift of discernment most often. I see people as they outwardly appear, but somehow I also see something significant about them. For example, a good friend of mine, a very wonderful man, came to me for help because he was a compulsive smoker. He loathed it, and he wanted to be free of it, but he could not; he was enslaved by it. I had tried everything in the book to help him and had approached it from every angle, but my help never lasted. He would get free for a couple of weeks and then go back to it. One day he phoned and said, "I'm flying in." He was coming halfway across the country, so I thought I had better come up with an answer. I didn't know anything more to do, so I said, "Let's go out and talk." We went and sat in a restaurant, and he began to tell me about his boyhood and things I had not known about him. He had gotten tired of his mother's religion and had run away from home. As he was telling me this, something looked out at me from within him and sort of said, "Do you see me?" And I saw something I had never seen before, because in the

Discernment is a form of direct perception, given by the Spirit.

natural, he was a well-behaved, polite, courteous man. Yet a little demon of rebellion had been there since his early boyhood. That night, we cast out that demon, and the smoking problem was solved. The smoking was just a branch on the trunk, but the trunk was rebellion.

There is therefore a way of seeing people that is not a vision and yet enables you to see what is important to a problem or situation. Discernment is very useful. Sometimes, it is also rather frightening and at times almost embarrassing to know what you wish you didn't know. We have to be prepared for this.

CULTIVATING DISCERNMENT

Hebrews 5:14 contains a very important fact about discernment that is also true, in various respects, about all the gifts.

Solid food belongs to those who are of full age [mature, grown up], *that is, those who by reason of use have their senses exercised to discern both good and evil.*

Very few of us begin operating in the gifts perfectly the first time. Yet we can practice and come to perfection in our understanding and operation of them. Some people are such perfectionists they will never do anything unless they know they can do it right the first time. This is a problem with many people concerning the exercise of the gifts of the Spirit. They think if they cannot prophesy like Isaiah, they will not prophesy at all. That really is absurd. Who knows how Isaiah began?

Discernment, particularly, can be cultivated. Hebrews 5:14 speaks about the necessity of exercising your senses to discern good and evil. To continue on your Christian journey always falling for every kind of trap Satan puts in your way is not to the glory of God. Neither is being unable to discern between the sincere person and the hypocrite. Many of us fail God by not exercising the discernment He has made available to us.

THE MEANING OF DISCERNINGS OF SPIRITS

Let us consider some definitions in regard to the gift of discernings of spirits. First, this gift does not refer only to discerning evil spirits. There are various classes of spirits that we encounter in the Christian life:

- the Holy Spirit, who is the Spirit of God

- good angels

- fallen, rebellious angels (demons or evil spirits)

- human spirits (every human being has his own spirit)

Second, as I mentioned earlier, the word *discernings* is in the plural. I believe this means each discerning is an operation of the gift. Similarly, with gifts of healings and workings of miracles, each healing or miracle is an operation of the gift.

Third, the gift of discernings of spirits is, again, operated under God's control. We cannot do it at will. At a convention in Fort Lauderdale, a woman wearing very dark glasses walked up to me at the end of a meeting. She stood right in front of me, and I wondered what was going to happen next. She whisked off her glasses and said, "Brother Prince, you have discernment. Look in my eyes and tell me if I have a demon." I said, "Sister, it doesn't work that way, I can't switch it on and switch it off at will. But if I'm ministering and I need the knowledge, then God will give it to me." She thought it was similar to an X-ray. It isn't like that. It is not under the control of the human will, although we have to be open to it or it will not come.

Manifestations of Discernings of Spirits in Scripture

Let us now consider some examples of the gift of discernings of spirits in the New Testament, according to the different categories of spirits I listed above.

Discerning the Holy Spirit

In the Form of a Dove

Earlier, we discussed how John the Baptist was given discernment through a vision. Let us look further at what he said about that vision.

> *The next day John saw Jesus coming toward him, and said, "Behold! The Lamb of God who takes away the sin of the world!...I did not know Him; but that He should be revealed to Israel, therefore I came baptizing with water." And John bore witness, saying, "I saw the Spirit descending from heaven like a dove, and He remained upon Him. I did not know Him, but He who sent me to baptize with water said to me, 'Upon whom you see the Spirit descending, and remaining on Him, this is He who baptizes with the Holy Spirit.'"* (John 1:29, 31–33)

Again, I think it is clear from the word of John the Baptist that only he saw the Holy Spirit descending like a dove. The rest of the people there did not see the vision. It was a supernatural discernment that was given specifically to John because he needed it. It was the way he would know who the Messiah was.

THE *Gifts* OF THE SPIRIT

AS TONGUES OF FIRE

In Acts 2, the Holy Spirit was manifested to human senses in the form of tongues of fire. *"Then there appeared to them [the followers of Jesus] divided tongues, as of fire, and one sat upon each of them. And they were all filled with the Holy Spirit and began to speak with other tongues, as the Spirit gave them utterance"* (vv. 3–4). This was a supernatural discerning of the Holy Spirit. The Holy Spirit Himself is not tongues of fire, but He was manifested in that way.

It is very important to learn to discern the move of the Spirit.

It is tremendously important that we learn to discern the Holy Spirit when believers meet together—when He moves, through whom He moves, and how He moves. We must be in a position to recognize Him. Otherwise, we will often miss what God is doing in a meeting. A certain manifestation of the Holy Spirit may move in. For instance, I have recently seen the spirit of healing move into a place and just take over. Almost anybody could be healed at such a time. And anybody could pray for someone, and he would be healed. I have seen groups of about half a dozen all praying at one time and people getting healed. Another time the spirit of miracles moved in and miracles were taking place. These were manifest, evident miracles.

Unless we discern the Holy Spirit in these ways, we will miss so much of what God wants to do. Our human agenda during a church service is to sing three hymns and a chorus, give the announcements, and then have the sermon. Yet, what if, in the middle of all this, the Spirit of God moved in and it was the time for healing? If we ignore Him, we will miss the healing He wants to give. Remember that Bartimaeus, the blind man, was begging by the side of the road when he heard a crowd of people and asked what was happening. When he was told Jesus of Nazareth was coming, he knew, *This is it. It is now or never.* He did not let anybody's program stop him from getting to the Lord. (See Mark 10:46–52.)

Similarly, there are times in our meetings when we must recognize it is the moment to receive. We have to discern the Holy Spirit and be willing to let human plans, ideas, and pre-conceptions take a back seat, or we will miss out. When Bartimaeus wanted to be healed, all the people who knew about religious protocol said, "Stop. Don't make a noise; don't disturb Jesus—He's too busy." And there will always be people with their religious protocol who say you must not conduct yourself differently from the way things have always been. Yet if you want what God has for you, you have to do it when God says to do it.

Apparently, the Spirit of God led King David, a mighty man of valor, to dance in front of the ark of the covenant with all his might. His wife, Michal, met him afterward with her religious protocol, saying, in effect, "You made a spectacle of yourself dancing in front of all those maidservants." David answered, "I wasn't dancing in front of the maidservants. I was dancing in front of the Lord. I will make even more of a spectacle of myself than that if the Lord tells me to." We read that Michal the critic never bore a child because she despised David in this way. (See 2 Samuel 6:14–16, 20–23.) Similarly, a critical spirit that refuses what the Holy Spirit is doing makes people spiritually barren. We have to be open to the Holy Spirit and His working among us.

Discerning Angels

ASCENDING AND DESCENDING ON THE SON OF MAN

Jesus said to Nathanael, *"Because I said to you, 'I saw you under the fig tree,' do you believe? You will see greater things than these....Most assuredly, I say to you, hereafter you shall see heaven open, and the angels of God ascending and descending upon the Son of Man"* (John 1:50–51). This is a reference to the discerning of angels.

IN THE GARDEN OF GETHSEMANE

Jesus Himself discerned the presence of God's angels. Near the end of His ministry, just before He was arrested and crucified, Jesus was praying in the garden of Gethsemane. As He prayed in agony, *"an angel appeared to Him from heaven, strengthening Him"* (Luke 22:43). It seems clear from this account that Jesus was the only one who saw that angel through spiritual discernment. Others were there, but they did not see it.

AT THE RESURRECTION

After Jesus was resurrected, Mary Magdalene saw an angel that neither the apostle John nor the apostle Peter could see.

Now on the first day of the week Mary Magdalene went to the tomb early, while it was still dark, and saw that the stone had been taken away from the tomb. Then she ran and came to Simon Peter, and to the other disciple [John], whom Jesus loved, and said to them, "They have taken away the Lord out of the tomb, and we do not know where they have laid Him." Peter therefore went out, and the other disciple, and were going to the tomb. So they both ran together, and the other disciple outran Peter and came to the tomb first. And he, stooping down and looking in, saw the linen cloths lying

there; yet he did not go in. Then Simon Peter came, follow-
ing him, and went into the tomb; and he saw the linen cloths
lying there, and the handkerchief that had been around His
head, not lying with the linen cloths, but folded together in
a place by itself. Then the other disciple, who came to the
tomb first, went in also; and he saw and believed. For as
yet they did not know the Scripture, that He must rise again
from the dead. Then the disciples went away again to their
own homes. But Mary stood outside by the tomb weeping,
and as she wept she stooped down and looked into the tomb.
And she saw two angels in white sitting, one at the head
and the other at the feet, where the body of Jesus had lain.

(John 20:1–12)

All Peter and John saw were the linen cloths and the handkerchief. Then they went back home. They did not see the
angels, but Mary did. She saw them through spiritual discernment.

In the children's home my wife
Lydia operated in Israel for many
years, there were times when the
small children would be conscious of
the presence of an angel the others
could not see. Once a little boy was
very sick, and my wife was trying to
nurse him back to health. She was sitting with the children in the kitchen
one day, and one of the girls lifted up
her head and said, "Mama, I saw an

**We may
discern angels
ministering to
us and carrying
out God's will.**

angel, and he came and took Joseph." The next day, Joseph
died. God had shown that little girl He was coming to take the
sick little boy to be with Him.

The *Gifts* of the Spirit

On a Perilous Journey at Sea

In the book of Acts, we read about Paul being transported as a prisoner on a ship that was *"exceedingly tempest-tossed"* (Acts 27:18) and about to be wrecked on the island of Malta. Paul stood up in the middle of the storm and told the rest of the people on board,

> *I urge you to take heart, for there will be no loss of life among you, but only of the ship. For there stood by me this night an angel of the God to whom I belong and whom I serve, saying, "Do not be afraid, Paul; you must be brought before Caesar; and indeed God has granted you all those who sail with you." Therefore take heart, men, for I believe God that it will be just as it was told me. However, we must run aground on a certain island.* (vv. 22–26)

The only person who was aware of the angel was Paul, and the angel's words were confirmed to be 100 percent accurate.

Discerning Human Spirits

Jesus and Nathanael

Then there is the discernment of human spirits. In connection with the word of knowledge, we have already looked at Jesus' supernatural revelation of Nathanael. However, let us return to that incident as an example of the discerning of human spirits as well. In John 1:47, we read, *"Jesus saw Nathanael coming toward Him, and said of him, 'Behold, an Israelite indeed, in whom is no deceit!'"* Jesus discerned a guileless spirit. This does not refer to a spirit other than Nathanael's, but to his own human spirit.

JESUS AND THE HEARTS OF MEN

Note what the Scripture says about Jesus in the second chapter of John:

> *Now when He was in Jerusalem at the Passover, during the feast, many believed in His name when they saw the signs which He did. But Jesus did not commit Himself to them, **because He knew all men**, and had no need that anyone should testify of man, **for He knew what was in man.*** (John 2:23–25, emphasis added)

Jesus was not deceived by people. He could see the invisible, real man inside the outer man. The rest of the disciples accepted Judas and had no idea he would be the one to betray Jesus. Jesus saw this from the beginning and yet made him an apostle because He was following His Father's purposes. (See John 6:64.)

PETER AND SIMON THE SORCERER

In Acts 8, Peter exercised the gift of discernment in dealing with Simon the sorcerer. Simon had long dominated the city of Samaria with his witchcraft and sorcery. When he heard Philip preaching the gospel and saw the miracles and signs he performed, he was baptized and became a disciple, in a sense. Then John and Peter came down and prayed for the converts, and they received the Holy Spirit with manifest evidence of power, through the laying on of the apostles' hands.

> *When Simon saw that through the laying on of the apostles' hands the Holy Spirit was given, he offered them money, saying, "Give me this power also, that anyone on whom I lay hands may receive the Holy Spirit." But Peter said to*

him, "Your money perish with you, because you thought that the gift of God could be purchased with money! You have neither part nor portion in this matter, for your heart is not right in the sight of God. Repent therefore of this your wickedness, and pray God if perhaps the thought of your heart may be forgiven you. For I see that you are poisoned by bitterness and bound by iniquity." (Acts 8:18–23)

Peter saw through the outward conformity of Simon to the inward crookedness and wrong motives in his heart. Apparently, Philip had not previously seen through Simon while he was there. A revelation of the inner nature of Simon was given to Peter.

PAUL AND THE FAITH OF THE CRIPPLED MAN

In Acts 14, we have an example of Paul discerning faith in a man who was crippled.

*And in Lystra a certain man without strength in his feet was sitting, a cripple from his mother's womb, who had never walked. This man heard Paul speaking. Paul, **observing him intently and seeing that he had faith to be healed**, said with a loud voice, "Stand up straight on your feet!" And he leaped and walked.*

(Acts 14:8–10, emphasis added)

Paul was in the middle of speaking to what was probably a large congregation when he looked at that one man and saw faith in him. He stopped in the middle of his message and said, *"Stand up straight on your feet!"* The man responded in faith and began to walk. This was not an instance of Paul discerning the Holy Spirit or the working of evil spirits, but rather the spirit of belief in a man. In 2 Corinthians 4:13, Paul spoke about the spirit of faith: *"And since we have the same spirit of faith, according to what is written, 'I believed and therefore I spoke,' we also believe and therefore speak."*

Discerning Evil Spirits

Let us now discuss the discerning of evil spirits. In the ministry of Jesus, this gift was frequently used in connection with healing. It is quite remarkable how often physical sickness in the gospel is attributed to evil spirits.

MUTENESS AND DEAFNESS CAUSED BY EVIL SPIRITS

The first example is Jesus' healing of a man who was mute.

> *As they went out, behold, they brought to Him a man, mute and demon-possessed. And when the demon was cast out, the mute spoke. And the multitudes marveled, saying, "It was never seen like this in Israel!"* (Matthew 9:32–33)

Jesus discerned the man's inability to speak was caused by an evil spirit that prevented him from using his vocal cords. When He cast out the evil spirit, the man immediately spoke. This is not to suggest evil spirits cause all muteness, but in this case, an evil spirit was behind it, and Jesus discerned that.

Jesus often discerned evil spirits in connection with sickness.

My wife Lydia and I witnessed cases where muteness immediately ceased when evil spirits were cast out.

In Kenya, East Africa, whenever an evangelist was ministering in a certain city there, the Asians who were Hindus would not come near a Christian church; they were not interested. But when an American evangelist came with a ministry of healing, they would line up or sit down on the grass and wait for hours before the meeting opened because healing is what they wanted.

The mayor of this city, a wealthy Asian, had a son who was eighteen years old and had never spoken. After an evil spirit was cast out of him, that young man immediately started imitating sounds and learning to speak. That incident made more impact on those Asians than ten years of normal missionary activity had. These things are real, but, again, I do not suggest for a moment that *all* dumbness or deafness is caused by evil spirits. Yet we must be able to discern when they are.

There is a similar example in the twelfth chapter of Matthew:

> *Then one was brought to Him who was demon-possessed, blind and mute; and He healed him, so that the blind and mute man both spoke and saw. And all the multitudes were amazed and said, "Could this be the Son of David?"*
> (Matthew 12:22–23)

It is clear from the context that Jesus healed this man by casting out an evil spirit that was causing his blindness and muteness.

Once we were ministering to a young woman in Atlanta, Georgia, and many evil spirits were coming out of her, naming themselves as they did. One was called "Blindness." When her husband heard this, he almost jumped. He said, "The doctor has told her that she'll be blind." I said, "She's not going to be blind now." A blind spirit will come in to produce blindness over a period of time, just as a deaf spirit will come in. It doesn't immediately produce total deafness, but the deafness will follow. It is the product of what the spirit does.

A woman I know well, who was stone-deaf in one ear, was in a meeting in London. An evangelist cast out a deaf spirit from her, and the woman heard everything with that ear perfectly, instantly. Yet she didn't have the faith to keep her healing. About two weeks later, she was as deaf as she had ever been. She allowed the spirit to come back. This is why it is so important for Christians to realize we have to identify the evil spirits we cast out. The Scripture says the devil is a murderer, and a murderer is one who kills physically. The devil will do this if we let him. He is a ruthless, unscrupulous, cruel enemy, and we have to understand what we are dealing with.

A further example may be seen in the book of Mark.

Then one of the crowd answered and said, "Teacher, I brought You my son, who has a mute spirit. And wherever it seizes him, it throws him down; he foams at the mouth, gnashes his teeth, and becomes rigid. So I spoke to Your disciples, that they should cast it out, but they could not." He answered him and said, "O faithless generation, how long shall I be with you? How long shall I bear with you? Bring him to Me." Then they brought him to Him. And when he saw Him, immediately the spirit convulsed him, and he fell on the ground and wallowed, foaming at the mouth. So He asked his father, "How long has this been happening to him?" And he said, "From childhood. And often he has thrown him both into the fire and into the water to destroy him. But if You can do anything, have compassion on us and help us." Jesus said to him, "If you can believe, all things are possible to him who believes." Immediately the father of the child cried out and said with tears, "Lord, I believe; help my unbelief!" When Jesus saw that the people came running together, He rebuked the unclean spirit, saying to it, "Deaf and dumb spirit, I command you, come out of him and enter him no more!" Then the spirit cried out, convulsed him greatly, and came out of him. And he became as one dead, so that many said, "He is dead." But Jesus took him by the hand and lifted him up, and he arose.

(Mark 9:17–27)

We should note several important truths revealed in this passage. First, Jesus did not tell the man, "This is too hard," or "This condition is the will of God for your son." Instead, He said, *"Bring him to Me."* That was Jesus' attitude about every single case of sickness. For example, when the centurion said, "I have a sick servant at home," Jesus said, "I'll come and heal him." (See Matthew 8:5–13; Luke 7:2–10.) There never was a question about the will of Jesus to heal and deliver, and we must understand His willingness to heal and deliver today.

Next, the boy's father told Jesus the evil spirit *"throws him down; he foams at the mouth, gnashes his teeth, and becomes rigid."* From this description, most people would say the boy had epilepsy, but there was something else happening that needed to be discerned.

Jesus asked the father, *"How long has this been happening to him?"* He answered, *"From childhood."* Childhood experiences are often crucial in tracing the origin and entrance of a demon.

The man told Jesus, *"If You can do anything, have compassion on us and help us."* Jesus' response was, *"If you can believe, all things are possible to him who believes."* He put the responsibility right back on the father. Many Christians do not recognize the spiritual responsibilities of parenthood. We are responsible to have faith for our children. Jesus did not say, "If your son can believe." He said, in effect, "If you can believe, your son can be healed." In Matthew 15, there was a Syrophoenician woman who had a daughter who was grievously tormented by an evil spirit, and she had faith for her daughter's healing. Jesus told her, *"Great is your faith!"* (v. 28) and her daughter was cured. (See Matthew 15:22–28.)

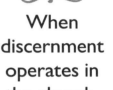

When discernment operates in the church, remarkable ministry follows.

In the case of this man and his son, "[Jesus] *rebuked the unclean spirit, saying to it, 'Deaf and dumb spirit, I command you, come out of him and enter him no more!' Then the spirit cried out, convulsed him greatly, and came out of him."*

Jesus specifically called the evil spirit a *"deaf and dumb spirit."* And when the spirit came out, the epilepsy ceased. This idea could be controversial, but epilepsy can be caused by an evil spirit. I have had an epileptic demon talk to me out of people. I have had one talk to me with a man's voice out of a woman's body. We have to discern and learn how to deal with evil spirits that cause sickness.

A Crippling Condition Caused by an Evil Spirit

Another example is a spirit of infirmity that plagued a woman for eighteen years. We read in Luke,

And behold, there was a woman who had a spirit of infirmity eighteen years, and was bent over and could in no

way raise herself up. But when Jesus saw her, He called her to Him and said to her, "Woman, you are loosed from your infirmity." And He laid His hands on her, and immediately she was made straight, and glorified God. But the ruler of the synagogue answered with indignation, because Jesus had healed on the Sabbath; and he said to the crowd, "There are six days on which men ought to work; therefore come and be healed on them, and not on the Sabbath day." The Lord then answered him and said, "Hypocrite! Does not each one of you on the Sabbath loose his ox or donkey from the stall, and lead it away to water it? So ought not this woman, being a daughter of Abraham, whom Satan has bound; think of it; for eighteen years, be loosed from this bond on the Sabbath?" And when He said these things, all His adversaries were put to shame; and all the multitude rejoiced for all the glorious things that were done by Him. (Luke 13:11–17)

What caused the woman's physical problem? A *"spirit of infirmity."* Jesus said that Satan had *"bound"* the woman. Notice that she was healed immediately after she was released from the power of the evil spirit. The moment the spirit left her, she could straighten her back. Jesus had to be able to discern the cause of her illness to know how to deal with it.

A Spirit of Divination

Our final example is an incident that occurred when Paul and Silas were preaching the gospel in Philippi.

Now it happened, as we went to prayer, that a certain slave girl possessed with a spirit of divination met us, who brought her masters much profit by fortune-telling. This girl

*followed Paul and us, and cried out, saying, "These men
are the servants of the Most High God, who proclaim to us
the way of salvation." And this she did for many days. But
Paul, greatly annoyed, turned and said to the spirit, "I command you in the name of Jesus Christ to come out of her."
And he came out that very hour.* (Acts 16:16–18)

Every word the girl said was true; she was advertising the
preachers of the gospel, but an evil spirit was doing it through
her. Paul discerned this and cast the spirit out of her. We must
have the same kind of discernment today. Fortune-telling
demons are rife in the church. Everywhere I go, even in nice
"respectable" church congregations, I encounter the demons
of sorcery, witchcraft, and divination among people who are
fooling around with horoscopes, Ouija boards, and astrology.
They become "hooked" by this same demon of divination.

RESULTS OF DISCERNINGS OF SPIRITS

The gift of discernings of spirits is very important to the
functioning of the body of Christ. It results in believers recognizing the presence of the Holy Spirit and the ways in which
God is working, it reveals the character and motivations of
human hearts, and it identifies when evil spirits are the cause
of sickness and strife. When discernings of spirits is operating
on a full scale in the body of Christ, it will bring remarkable
ministry to the church and world.

PART 3

Gifts OF POWER

CHAPTER 7

We move on now to the gifts of power—faith, gifts of healings, and workings of miracles. As we begin with the gift of faith, let us clarify the nature of this gift by noting the differences between three kinds of faith referred to in the New Testament.

DIFFERENT KINDS OF FAITH

Faith for Salvation

First, Romans 10:17 says, *"Faith comes by hearing, and hearing by the word of God."* This is the faith that a person receives through hearing the preaching of the gospel of Jesus Christ. As a person opens his heart and receives this word, it produces faith within him. This kind of faith is necessary for salvation. In Ephesians 2:8–9, Paul stated regarding the requirement for salvation, *"For by grace you have been saved through faith, and that not of yourselves; it is the gift of God, not of works, lest anyone should boast."* The grace of God that brings salvation comes to us through faith. We cannot boast about this faith, however, because God gave it to us as we opened our hearts to hear the preaching of the gospel.

The fact that faith is absolutely essential for salvation is also emphasized in several other passages of Scripture. The first is Romans 4:4–5: *"Now to him who works, the wages are not counted as grace but as debt. But to him who does not work but believes on Him who justifies the ungodly, his faith is accounted for righteousness."* In order to receive righteousness, we must have faith. Our faith in Jesus Christ, which comes through the hearing of the gospel, is imputed to us by God as righteousness.

Paul wrote, *"For I say, through the grace given to me, to everyone who is among you, not to think of himself more highly than he ought to think, but to think soberly, as God has dealt to each one a measure of faith"* (Romans 12:3). Paul did not say "the" measure of faith but "a" measure of faith. God has given to each believer a certain proportion of faith. This is what is often called "saving faith" or faith for salvation or faith that accompanies salvation.

This truth is also implied in Hebrews 11:6: *"Without faith it is impossible to please* [God], *for he who comes to God must believe that He is, and that He is a rewarder of those who diligently seek Him."* No one can please God, no one can approach God, and no one can receive salvation without the faith that comes by hearing His Word.

Faith as a Fruit of the Holy Spirit

The second kind of faith is part of the fruit of the Holy Spirit: *"the fruit of the Spirit is love, joy, peace, longsuffering, gentleness, goodness, faith, meekness, temperance: against such there is no law"* (Galatians 5:22–23 KJV). We have already noted the fruit of the Spirit is ninefold, just as the gifts of the Spirit are ninefold. I think it is one of the marks of the beautiful inspiration of the Holy Spirit that there is an exact balance between the gifts and the fruit. I personally believe all the fruit of the Spirit is love, but love manifests itself in various aspects.

The seventh fruit of the Spirit is *"faith"* (Galatians 5:22 KJV). This is not the type of faith we must have to be saved. Every one of the ninefold forms of the fruit of the Spirit is a mark of character. This faith means "continuing quiet trust" or "dependability" or "faithfulness." If a person has continuing quiet trust, he does not become flustered or overemotional in any circumstance. Very few people have this quality the moment they are saved. It comes by experience and cultivation. A dependable and faithful person is reliable; he keeps his commitments. He is someone you can put your trust in. If he says he will take a Sunday school class, he will be there every week to teach the Sunday school class. So this faith denotes an aspect of character.

The gift of faith that comes from the Holy Spirit is miraculous faith.

MIRACULOUS FAITH

The third kind of faith, which is one of the gifts of the Holy Spirit, is miraculous faith. *"To another* [is given] *faith by the same Spirit"* (1 Corinthians 12:9). I pointed out previously that God has all wisdom, but He doesn't give us all that wisdom at once. In a moment of need, He imparts to us a word of His wisdom by the Holy Spirit. This is just a little fragment of His wisdom that meets the need of that situation. Similarly, although God has all knowledge, He does not impart to us all that knowledge because we would stagger under the load.

Again, in the moment of need, He imparts to us a word of His knowledge by the Holy Spirit. He imparts the gift of faith in a very similar way.

Paul did not say God gives "a word" of faith, but this is essentially what it is. God has all faith, and through this gift He imparts to us a tiny portion of it. It is not human faith or faith that is cultivated. It is divine faith. This is faith that comes instantly, supernaturally, as a gift directly from God by the Holy Spirit, very frequently in the form of a word. This gift, like the others we have examined so far, is operated only under God's control. No one has a word of knowledge or a word of wisdom at will. No one discerns spirits at will. Likewise, no one has the gift of faith at will. These gifts remain under God's control, but we make ourselves available to Him so He may operate them through us as He desires.

If all believers could operate the gift of faith at any time, the world would be in chaos and confusion because we would use it to suit our own moods and needs. One person would be moving the mountain east while the other was moving the mountain west. There are certain gifts God has to keep very strict control over, and faith is definitely one of them.

THE NATURE OF GOD'S FAITH

Miraculous faith is therefore the impartation of divine faith to humanity. Let us look for a moment at the nature of God's faith.

The faith of God is a fascinating study. His faith in His own word brought the entire universe into being. Psalm 33:6 says, *"By the word of the LORD the heavens were made, and all the host of them by the breath of His mouth."*

The image of God's "breath" is important. I took a course in phonetics and discovered some remarkable things. It is impossible for a person to speak without breathing. When a word goes out of your mouth, your breath also goes out with it. Essentially, every form of speech, in all the languages of the world, is just a variation on the way air comes out of our mouths. When you think of the uncountable number of variations and what is achieved by them, it is really fascinating to contemplate. In Psalm 33:6, the Hebrew word translated as *"breath"* means "spirit." "By the word of the Lord the heavens were made, and all the host of them by the spirit of His mouth." In other words, all creation is the product of God's Word and God's Spirit going forth together. Or, God's word going forth *through* His Spirit. Therefore, when God speaks, His breath, His Spirit, goes with it. The breathed-out word of God produced all that was ever created.

All creation is the product of God's Word and God's Spirit going forth together.

Let us look at some Scripture passages that confirm this truth. In Genesis 1:2, we read, *"The Spirit of God was hovering over the face of the waters."* What was the next thing that happened? *"God said, 'Let there be light'; and there was light"* (v. 3). God's word went out of His mouth, and when the word and the Spirit of God united, the word *light* turned into the thing called light. In both Hebrew and Greek the same words for "word" are used for "thing." This is no accident, because things are God's words spoken into being by His Spirit. When God said "light," there was light. This is the origin and nature of all creation.

In Hebrews 11:3, the same truth is presented again in relation to God's word breathed forth by His Spirit. *"By faith we understand that the worlds* [the ages] *were framed* [fitted together] *by the word of God, so that the things which are seen were not made of things which are visible."* What is the basic force behind all created things? It is the word of God by the Spirit of God.

I once studied the philosophy of physics. As I understand it, if you were to ask a physicist what a certain desk was made of, he would give you an answer in terms of atoms. If you were to ask him what atoms are made of, he would give you an answer in terms of protons, neutrons, and electrons. If you were to ask him if anybody has ever seen any of these things, the answer would be no. If you were to ask him to express any of these realities, the best he could do would be to give you some kind of mathematical formula or equation. He would essentially be in agreement with the writer of Hebrews who, nineteen centuries ago, wrote, *"The things which are seen were not made of things which are visible."* What is now visible, tangible, or perceptible was not made of things we can see.

It is impossible to *over*estimate the immense power of words, though most Christians sadly *under*estimate them. Ezekiel 12:25 says, *"For I am the LORD. I speak, and the word which I speak will come to pass."* In other words, "I am God, and when I say something, it happens." This is God's unchanging, eternal nature. We immediately see the possibility that, if the breath of the Spirit of God is within us, that same breath can bring forth a word from us that is just as effective as if almighty God had spoken it directly.

This is exactly what the gift of faith is.

SPEAKING THE WORD IN FAITH

Let us look at some of the teachings of Jesus in this connection. We will begin by comparing the two gospel versions of the incident of the fig tree Jesus cursed. In Matthew 21:18–22, we read,

> *Now in the morning, as He returned to the city, He was hungry. And seeing a fig tree by the road, He came to it and found nothing on it but leaves, and said to it, "Let no fruit grow on you ever again." Immediately the fig tree withered away. And when the disciples saw it, they marveled, saying, "How did the fig tree wither away so soon?" So Jesus answered and said to them, "Assuredly, I say to you, if you have faith and do not doubt, you will not only do what was done to the fig tree, but also if you say to this mountain, 'Be removed and be cast into the sea,' it will be done. And whatever things you ask in prayer, believing, you will receive."*

There are two ways of using words, which are brought out in this passage. One way is toward something or someone on behalf of God, and the other way is toward God on behalf of something or someone. First, Jesus did not pray *about* the fig tree and He did not pray *to* the fig tree, which would have been idolatry. He *spoke* to the fig tree on behalf of God, and the fig tree did what He told it to do. Jesus told His disciples they could do what was done to the fig tree if they had faith. What's more, if they spoke to a mountain, it would have to obey them just the same. Second, Jesus explained to His disciples that if you are in prayer to God on behalf of something, whatever you ask in prayer believing, you will receive. I will discuss these two ways of using words in more detail later in the chapter.

But according to the leading of the Holy Spirit, you may either speak to something on behalf of God or you may speak to God on behalf of something.

Now let us look at the same incident as recorded in Mark, because this account includes something further Jesus said that really is the key to understanding it all.

> *The next day, when they had come out from Bethany, He was hungry. And seeing from afar a fig tree having leaves, He went to see if perhaps He would find something on it. When He came to it, He found nothing but leaves, for it was not the season for figs. In response Jesus said to it, "Let no one eat fruit from you ever again." And His disciples heard it....Now in the morning, as they passed by, they saw the fig tree dried up from the roots. And Peter, remembering, said to Him, "Rabbi, look! The fig tree which You cursed has withered away." So Jesus answered and said to them, "Have faith in God."* (Mark 11:12–14, 20–22)

The literal translation of Jesus' statement is "Have the faith of God." Again, God's faith expressed through the words of human beings are just as authoritative as if God Himself had spoken them. In a certain sense, since they are breathed forth by the Spirit of God, they are God-given utterances. Jesus went on to say,

> *For assuredly, I say to you, whoever says to this mountain, "Be removed and be cast into the sea," and does not doubt in his heart, but believes that those things he says will be done, he will have whatever he says. Therefore I say to you, whatever things you ask when you pray, believe that you receive them, and you will have them.* (vv. 23–24)

If we take the opening and closing words of verse twenty-three, we have the most remarkable truth: "Whoever says...will have whatever he says." This does not leave anybody or anything out. It is *whoever* and *whatever*. The condition is to have divine faith—the faith of God. The suggestion is that God is more willing to give us this faith than many of us are to receive it. Jesus was saying, "Do not marvel. You can do it. Have the faith of God."

In 1 Corinthians 13, Paul listed a number of spiritual gifts, including faith, the mountain-moving gift:

> *Though I speak with the tongues of men and of angels, but have not love, I have become sounding brass or a clanging cymbal. And though I have the gift of prophecy, and understand all mysteries [word of wisdom] and all knowledge [word of knowledge], and though I have all faith, so that I could remove mountains....* (vv. 1–2)

You do not lay hands on a mountain, and you do not perform a miracle over it; you just speak to a mountain. If you speak with divine faith, that mountain has to do what you tell it to do.

If you speak with divine faith, the mountain has to do what you say.

Note Jesus' statement about prayer: *"Therefore I say to you, whatever things you ask when you pray, believe that you receive them, and you will have them"* (Mark 11:24). I often ask people, "When do you receive?" The answer is, "When you pray." The moment you pray, you receive. *Having* may come later, but *receiving* comes when you pray. This is the great secret to obtaining things. The devil always has a tomorrow, and if you let him keep you at bay with his tomorrows, you will never receive what God has for you. The Bible says that, as far as God is concerned, *"Now is the accepted time; behold, now is the day of salvation"* (2 Corinthians 6:2). God lives in an eternal now.

DIVINE MUSTARD-SEED FAITH

In Matthew, we read about the disciples' inability to cast out a demon from an epileptic boy. When they were alone with Jesus, they asked Him, *"Why could we not cast it out?"* (Matthew 17:19). Jesus had one simple answer: *"Because of your unbelief"* (v. 20). Then He went on to say,

> *Assuredly, I say to you, if you have faith as a mustard seed, you will say to this mountain, "Move from here to there," and it will move; and nothing will be impossible for you. However, this kind does not go out except by prayer and fasting.* (vv. 20–21)

Let's compare this passage with Luke 17:6.

> *If you have faith as a mustard seed, you can say to this mulberry tree, "Be pulled up by the roots and be planted in the sea," and it would obey you.*

Notice the tree is not just cast into the sea but is *planted* in the sea. In both passages, the Lord says all you need is a "mustard seed" of this kind of faith for it to be effective. One little mustard seed is sufficient to move a mountain. If it is God's faith, you do not need a large spoonful of it. That is not true of every kind of faith, but this is divine faith. It is not the quantity but the quality of faith Jesus is speaking about.

THE *Gifts* OF THE SPIRIT

When I was planning to marry my wife Lydia, I was walking along the Mount of Olives and contemplating what would be involved in becoming a faith missionary in the land of Israel. Lydia had told me some stories about having to get up in the middle of the night to pray to receive the children's breakfast the next morning. I told the Lord I never wanted to be brought as close to the margin as that, and I settled the matter forever with God in faith. I knew things would never get to that point. When I look back at that time of prayer now, I know that is when I received. It wasn't a struggle; it wasn't an effort. I just knew that was the way it was going to be. And it was that way for thirty years of married life. I cannot take any credit for it. I mention it because I want you to see there can be a moment when God drops a mustard seed of divine faith into your heart and it is settled.

THE WORD IN THE HEART AND MOUTH

A very dramatic example of the faith of God and its power is illustrated in the calling of the prophet Jeremiah. God said to him, *"Before I formed you in the womb I knew you; before you were born I sanctified you; I ordained you a prophet to the nations"* (Jeremiah 1:5). Jeremiah replied, in effect, "I can't. I'm too young." And God essentially said, "Do not tell Me you are too young because you are going to do it." (See verses 6–8.) The passage continues,

> Then the LORD put forth His hand and touched my mouth, and the LORD said to me: "Behold, **I have put My words in your mouth**. See, I have this day set you over the nations and over the kingdoms, to root out and to pull down, to destroy and to throw down, to build and to plant."
>
> (vv. 9–10, emphasis added)

116

Jeremiah thought he was too young to be a prophet, but God told him, "From now on, you will be over the nations and over the kingdoms to root out, pull down, destroy, throw down, build, and plant." How was this achieved? *"I have put My words in your mouth"* (Jeremiah 1:9). And when God's words went forth from Jeremiah's mouth by God's Spirit, it was just as effective as if God Himself had spoken them. If you study the prophecies of Jeremiah, you will find that the destinies of many nations for the past 2,500 years were settled by his prophecies. They were exactly fulfilled. That is the power of the Word of God spoken by the human mouth through the Spirit of God.

The condition for being a mouth-piece of God is given in Jeremiah 15. Jeremiah's testimony was, *"Your words were found, and I ate them, and Your word was to me the joy and rejoicing of my heart; for I am called by Your name, O LORD God of hosts"* (v. 16). If we are to bring forth God's Word, we must first have digested God's Word. Likewise, when God called the prophet Ezekiel, He held out a roll in His hand and

To bring forth God's Word, we must first have digested God's Word.

said, *"Open your mouth and eat what I give you"* (Ezekiel 2:8). Then He told Ezekiel to prophesy.

We must fully understand that prophecy and spiritual gifts do not come out of the natural mind. We are not only to get the Word of God into our minds, but we are also to digest it in our spirits. When the Word is digested there, and we have hidden it in our hearts, as David said (see Psalm 119:11), then it is available for the Holy Spirit to bring forth as He sees fit. When Jeremiah received God's words, he ate them and lived on them. Likewise, the testimony of Job was, *"I have treasured the words of His mouth more than my necessary food"* (Job 23:12).

When I was newly saved and serving as a soldier in the British army in North Africa, this was my testimony as well. I preferred the Word of God to my food. If it came to a choice between eating breakfast and reading the Bible, I would take the time to read the Bible. For about three years in the desert, I lived on God's Word. There were no churches, chaplains, or preachers there, but I had two things: the Word and the Spirit of God. That experience made the most profound and permanent changes in every area of my being.

Finally, Jeremiah 15:19 says, *"Therefore thus says the LORD: 'If you return, then I will bring you back; you shall stand before Me; if you take out the precious from the vile, you shall be as My mouth. Let them return to you, but you must not return to them."* Jeremiah was to stand before God, hear His word, and deliver it. God wants a pure mouthpiece. When God sets a standard, we cannot lower it. When God sets conditions, we have no authority to change them. We cannot go down to man's standards. We have to stand where God sets us and let men return to His standards; we cannot return to theirs.

TWO WAYS OF USING WORDS IN FAITH

Earlier I mentioned two different ways of using words while exercising faith. The first way is words spoken to a person, object, or situation on behalf of God. This expression of faith does not have a theological name that I know of, but I would say it is the power of the believer's decree.

The second way is words spoken to God on behalf of a person, object, or situation. This expression of faith is what we call prayer.

The Example of Elijah

One of my favorite Bible characters, Elijah, illustrates both of these ways of using words while exercising faith. He emerged as a prophet in Israel at a time of total backsliding, evil, and chaos in the kingdom, which was being ruled by the wicked King Ahab. Elijah gave this dramatic utterance on behalf of God:

> *And Elijah the Tishbite, of the inhabitants of Gilead, said to Ahab, "As the LORD God of Israel lives, before whom I stand, there shall not be dew nor rain these years, except at my word."* (1 Kings 17:1)

That is quite a powerful statement, isn't it? When you control the rain and the dew, that's authority. The Bible reveals that for three and a half years, there was no rain and no dew, just as Elijah had said. Ahab sent to every kingdom and nation looking for Elijah. (See 1 Kings 18:10.) He apparently thought if he could get hold of Elijah and somehow torture him into saying the right thing, the rain would fall again. When they finally met, Ahab said to Elijah, *"Is that you, O troubler of Israel?"* (1 Kings 18:17). He was saying, "You're the one who is causing all this trouble; you're the reason why we don't have rain and dew; you're the reason why all the crops are failing and all the beasts are dying."

Speaking a word such as Elijah did is a responsibility. The weather was under the control of Elijah's word, not God's, because he was the visible representative of God to Israel. In 1 Kings 18:1, God had told Elijah, *"Go, present yourself to Ahab, and I will send rain on the earth."* Elijah did not just take the message to Ahab—he *was* the message. *"Present yourself...and I will send rain."*

Yet note that when Elijah wanted the rain again, he had to persevere in prayer about it, even though he was the one who had withheld it:

> *Then Elijah said to Ahab, "Go up, eat and drink; for there is the sound of abundance of rain." So Ahab went up to eat and drink. And Elijah went up to the top of Carmel; then he bowed down on the ground, and put his face between his knees.* (1 Kings 18:41–42)

The whole of Elijah was a prayer: spirit, soul, and body.

Have you ever been in that position? There have been times when I felt God had bent me into that position in prayer. I would not just say Elijah was praying, but that Elijah *was* his prayer. The whole of Elijah was a prayer: spirit, soul, and body. He was totally identified with his prayer. He prayed until the little cloud appeared, and by his words spoken to God, he liberated the rain. (See verses 43–45.)

This is what James called *"the prayer of faith"* (James 5:15). James used Elijah as an example, saying he was not a special kind of person but was a human being who was just like you and me. In other words, we can do the same.

> *The prayer of faith will save the sick, and the Lord will raise him up. And if he has committed sins, he will be forgiven….The effective, fervent prayer of a righteous man avails much. Elijah was a man with a nature like ours, and he prayed earnestly that it would not rain; and it did not rain on the land for three years and six months. And*

he prayed again, and the heaven gave rain, and the earth
produced its fruit.   (James 5:15–18)

This same power is available to you and me.

In the above Scripture, we are told that Elijah prayed in conjunction with speaking words on behalf of God. This shows us these two ways of using words while exercising faith are closely related. We do not just speak words on behalf of God arbitrarily; rather, we speak words in faith based on our relationship with Him and according to our knowledge of His will and power.

The Example of Joshua

Another example of a word spoken on behalf of God may be found in the life of Joshua, when he and the Israelites were in the middle of a battle against their enemies.

Then Joshua spoke to the LORD in the day when the LORD
delivered up the Amorites before the children of Israel, and
he said in the sight of Israel: "Sun, stand still over Gibeon;
and Moon, in the Valley of Aijalon." So the sun stood still,
and the moon stopped, till the people had revenge upon their
enemies....So the sun stood still in the midst of heaven, and
did not hasten to go down for about a whole day. And there
has been no day like that, before it or after it, that the LORD
heeded the voice of a man.   (Joshua 10:12–14)

Although the passage says Joshua spoke to the Lord, it was Joshua who told the sun and the moon to stand still. The words a man spoke affected the course of the heavenly bodies. This was remarkable. My personal conviction is that exactly the same privileges are available to you and me today.

MANIFESTATIONS OF MIRACULOUS FAITH IN THE NEW TESTAMENT

Let us now look at some examples of miraculous faith, or the word of faith, found in the New Testament.

Calming a Storm in Divine Authority

In the first example, Jesus and His disciples were in a small boat when a tremendous storm arose.

When evening had come, He said to them, "Let us cross over to the other side." Now when they had left the multitude, they took Him along in the boat as He was. And other little boats were also with Him. And a great windstorm arose, and the waves beat into the boat, so that it was already filling. But He was in the stern, asleep on a pillow. And they awoke Him and said to Him, "Teacher, do You not care that we are perishing?" Then He arose and rebuked the wind, and said to the sea, "Peace, be still!" And the wind ceased and there was a great calm. But He said to them, "Why are you so fearful? How is it that you have no faith?" And they feared exceedingly, and said to one another, "Who can this be, that even the wind and the sea obey Him!"

(Mark 4:35–41)

Jesus did not lay His hands on the sea—He just spoke to it. This is an example of divine authority through the word of faith. In the Greek, the literal meaning of the word translated *"be still"* is "be muzzled." It appears to me Jesus saw something satanic behind that sudden, abnormal, dramatic storm. He was on His way to what I consider His toughest case of deliverance, the Gadarene demoniac whom He met on the other side. I cannot but believe that all Satan's forces ganged up against

Him to prevent Him from getting to the scene of that man's deliverance. Sometimes, when we are on a particular assignment that means a great deal to the kingdom of God, Satan will have his agents planted in every situation and circumstance along the way. This is a good sign God is going to do something special, if we do not become discouraged and lose the victory on the way.

When Jesus spoke in divine authority, the storm was muzzled immediately. It could not utter another sound or cause any more damage. When Israel left Egypt on the Passover night, the Scripture says not a dog wagged its tongue at any of the Israelites. (See Exodus 11:7.) God can silence anything if we have faith.

Raising the Dead by a Word of Faith

There are three instances in the Scriptures of Jesus raising people from the dead by a word of faith. The first is the son of the widow of Nain.

> *And when He came near the gate of the city, behold, a dead man was being carried out, the only son of his mother; and she was a widow. And a large crowd from the city was with her. When the Lord saw her, He had compassion on her and said to her, "Do not weep." Then He came and touched the open coffin, and those who carried him stood still. And He said, "Young man, I say to you, arise." So he who was dead sat up and began to speak. And He presented him to his mother.* (Luke 7:12–15)

Jesus was moved by the woman's tragic situation and told her not to weep. This was divine compassion. A sure evidence that God wants to do something is when you are moved with divine compassion. Jesus spoke a word of faith and told the young man to arise.

Every time Jesus raised the dead, He was very specific. He always called to the person who was to be raised. Some people believe that if He had not designated the person, all the dead would have arisen because He had the power to call them all out of the grave.

The second instance concerns the daughter of Jairus.

Now all wept and mourned for her; but He said, "Do not weep; she is not dead, but sleeping." And they ridiculed Him, knowing that she was dead. But He put them all outside, took her by the hand and called, saying, "Little girl, arise." Then her spirit returned, and she arose immediately. And He commanded that she be given something to eat.

(Luke 8:52–55)

Again, Jesus spoke a word of faith and told the little girl to arise. Some people claim raising the dead never happens today. Yet, in East Africa, where my wife Lydia and I worked as missionaries, there have been well-authenticated cases of people being raised. During the time we worked there, there were two occasions in which someone was brought back from death. One involved a woman student of ours who had died. Her whole family was in the clinic next to her body, which was stretched out on the bed. They were weeping and wailing and praying. We asked if they would like us to pray, and they

Divine compassion is a sure evidence God wants to do something.

said yes. We asked them all to leave, and though we had not planned anything beforehand, we just knelt down on either side of the bed and prayed. At a certain moment we both received the assurance of victory, and the girl sat straight up.

The first thing she said was, "Has anybody got a Bible?" I said yes, and she told me to read Psalm 41. After I read Psalm 41, we took her home with us and she was perfectly well within a day or two. Later, I asked her, "Why did you want us to read Psalm 41?" She said, "At that time two men in white stood beside me and I walked, with them on either side, down a very, very long, straight pathway. It took us to a place that was full of lights and people in white clothing all singing. There was a man reading out of a very big book. He was reading Psalm 41, and I wanted to know what was in it." By the words of this psalm, we may see an example of the connection between the Word of God and miraculous faith:

> *The LORD will preserve him and keep him alive, and he will be blessed on the earth; you will not deliver him to the will of his enemies. The LORD will strengthen him on his bed of illness; you will sustain him on his sickbed. I said, "LORD, be merciful to me; heal my soul, for I have sinned against You." My enemies speak evil of me: "When will he die, and his name perish?"...All who hate me whisper together against me; against me they devise my hurt. "An evil disease," they say, "clings to him. And now that he lies down, he will rise up no more."...But You, O LORD, be merciful to me, and raise me up.* (Psalm 41:2–5, 7–8, 10)

The third instance is when Jesus raised Lazarus from the dead.

Then they took away the stone from the place where the dead man was lying. And Jesus lifted up His eyes and said, "Father, I thank You that You have heard Me. And I know that You always hear Me, but because of the people who are standing by I said this, that they may believe that You sent Me." Now when He had said these things, He cried with a loud voice, "Lazarus, come forth!" And he who had died came out bound hand and foot with graveclothes, and his face was wrapped with a cloth. Jesus said to them, "Loose him, and let him go."   (John 11:41–44)

What a dramatic moment. Notice that, in every case, Jesus spoke and told the person to rise. A similar occurrence happened when Peter raised Dorcas from the dead after her body had been washed and laid out in preparation for burial:

All the widows stood by [Peter] weeping, showing the tunics and garments which Dorcas had made while she was with them. But Peter put them all out, and knelt down and prayed. And turning to the body he said, "Tabitha, arise." And she opened her eyes, and when she saw Peter she sat up. Then he gave her his hand and lifted her up; and when he had called the saints and widows, he presented her alive.
(Acts 9:39–41)

Notice Peter was specific, as Jesus had been, and called her by name. After praying and receiving the word of faith, he told Tabitha to rise, and she did.

SPEAKING JUDGMENT THROUGH A WORD OF FAITH

Our final example is a very remarkable situation from the book of Acts. Elymas the sorcerer—a false prophet or magician—opposed the preaching of Paul and Barnabas on the island of Cyprus.

> *Then Saul, who also is called Paul, filled with the Holy*
> *Spirit, looked intently at him and said, "O full of all deceit*
> *and all fraud, you son of the devil, you enemy of all righ-*
> *teousness, will you not cease perverting the straight ways of*
> *the Lord? And now, indeed, the hand of the Lord is upon*
> *you, and you shall be blind, not seeing the sun for a time."*
> *And immediately a dark mist fell on him, and he went*
> *around seeking someone to lead him by the hand.*
>
> (Acts 13:9–11)

Paul pronounced God's judgment on Elymas through the power of the spoken word. Notice Paul was *"filled with the Holy Spirit,"* revealing the judgment came through a divine word of faith.

RESULTS OF MIRACULOUS FAITH

When God imparts divine faith to humanity, human beings can speak forth the same results as if God had spoken the words directly. Those to whom divine faith comes have allowed the Word of God to penetrate past their minds and into their spirits and hearts, from which miraculous words of faith come according to the leading of the Holy Spirit. These words have power over creation, death, and Satan, demonstrating author-ity in all aspects of physical and spiritual existence. They tear down evil and build up what is good and righteous by the faith of God Himself.

CHAPTER 8

GIFTS OF

n the next two chapters, we will explore gifts of healings and workings of miracles. To gain an overall perspective of these two gifts, we should note the distinction between a healing and a miracle.

DISTINGUISHING BETWEEN HEALINGS AND MIRACLES

Essentially, a healing relieves the body of disease or injury. It is often imperceptible to the senses. It may also be gradual; it does not necessarily happen instantaneously or even in a very short period of time. On the other hand, a miracle is usually perceptible to the senses and almost instantaneous, and it produces a change that goes beyond healing.

For instance, you cannot "heal" one leg that is shorter than the other, but God can lengthen it. I have seen thousands of cases in which legs have grown out instantaneously and visibly after prayer. I have also witnessed the restoration of an ear. A man who asked for prayer for the healing of his ear mentioned afterward that his inner ear had been surgically removed. When he went back to a doctor and had his ear examined, the doctor told him he had a completely normal ear. This was not just a healing because you cannot heal something that is not there. This was a creative or restorative miracle.

Of course, healing and miracles can overlap one other. An instantaneous healing that is visible could be described as a miracle. I have witnessed quite a number of these healings. Once I prayed for a girl who had acne. I didn't really expect much, but in the next ten minutes, her face changed to a kind of glowing pink. It was absolutely supernatural. All that was left was a faint shadow where the spots had been. That was a healing, but it was so perceptible and instantaneous you might call it a miracle.

THE NATURE OF GIFTS OF HEALINGS

We will now look in a more in-depth way at gifts of healings. *"To another* [is given] *gifts of healings by the same Spirit"* (1 Corinthians 12:9). Again, with this gift, both *gifts* and *healings* are in the plural. I interpret this to mean each time a healing comes, it is a gift given through the person by whom the gift is manifested.

Under God's Control

As with other gifts of the Spirit, gifts of healings are operated only under God's control. I do not believe anyone can go around healing people at will anywhere and at any time. If you manifest gifts of healings, some foolish person may say to you, "Walk into the hospital and heal everybody." That is really unscriptural. For example, look at the incident in which Jesus healed the invalid man at the pool of Bethesda.

Now there is in Jerusalem by the Sheep Gate a pool, which is called in Hebrew, Bethesda, having five porches. In these lay a great multitude of sick people, blind, lame, paralyzed....Now a certain man was there who had an infirmity thirty-eight years. When Jesus saw him lying there, and knew that he already had been in that condition a long time, He said to him, "Do you want to be made well?" The sick man answered Him, "Sir, I have no man to put me into the pool when the water is stirred up; but while I am coming, another steps down before me." Jesus said to him, "Rise, take up your bed and walk." And immediately the man was made well, took up his bed, and walked. (John 5:2–3, 5–9)

"Do you want to be made well?" might seem like a strange question to ask a man who had been there for thirty-eight years seeking healing. However, the exercise of the will can be an important factor in being healed.

> Jesus Himself could not operate independently of the Father's will.

Note there was a great multitude of sick people at the pool. Yet Jesus went in, healed one man, and walked out again. When Jesus was questioned about the healing, He said, *"Most assuredly, I say to you, the Son can do nothing of Himself, but what He sees the Father do; for whatever He does, the Son also does in like manner"* (v. 19). Jesus did not claim the ability to do anything independently of the Father. In another place He said, *"The words that I speak to you I do not speak on My own authority; but the Father who dwells in Me does the works"* (John 14:10). In other words, Jesus Himself could not go out and do anything in His own will or by His own decision if it was not by revelation of the Father's will. Jesus did not operate in that way, and we cannot either.

We must be directed by God in these matters. For example, when fifty people come forward in a meeting for healing, it is usually very unsatisfactory to line them up, give them a number, and start with number one. The first person in line may be someone who has no faith, so you pray for him and nothing happens. Number two may also have no faith. By the time you pray for him and nothing happens, *nobody* has any faith. You're fighting unbelief in everybody. We have learned by experience to let the Lord select the one to begin with. We can only do these things insofar as God leads us and operates through us, as He did through Jesus and the apostles.

The Power of the Spirit for the Believer's Body

Healing power is the power of the Holy Spirit made available to the body of the believer. In Romans 8:11, Paul wrote, *"But if the Spirit of Him who raised Jesus from the dead dwells in you, He who raised Christ from the dead will also give life to your mortal bodies through His Spirit who dwells in you."* You have available within you, through the indwelling Holy Spirit, the very same power that raised to life the dead body of Jesus. Paul brought out the same idea when he gave this testimony:

> *Always carrying about in the body the dying of the Lord Jesus, that the life of Jesus also may be manifested in our body. For we who live are always delivered to death for Jesus' sake, that the life of Jesus also may be manifested in our mortal flesh. So then death is working in us, but life in you.* (2 Corinthians 4:10–12)

We do not yet have our resurrection bodies. But what we do have, and what we are entitled to claim, is resurrection life in a mortal body. The resurrection life of Jesus Christ is made available to the body of the believer by the Holy Spirit through faith. Paul said, *"That the life of Jesus also may be manifested in our mortal flesh."* The life is not just to be there, but it is also to be made manifest. This is what I call divine healing and divine health. It is the presence of the Spirit of God that raised the body of Jesus out of the tomb made manifest, operating so that you can see it is present and observe what it is doing. James wrote, *"Is anyone among you sick? Let him call for the elders of the church, and let them pray over him, anointing him with oil in the name of the Lord"* (James 5:14). The oil typifies the Holy Spirit giving resurrection life to the body of the believer.

The will of God for the believer is not just to be healed, but to be healthy.

I believe the resurrection life goes beyond healing to health. The will of God is not for the believer in Christ to keep getting healed but to be healthy. His will for the believer is stated in 3 John 2: *"Beloved, I pray that you may prosper in all things and be in health, just as your soul prospers."* I have learned by experience it is much easier to be in health than it is to keep getting healed. It is good to be healed, but it is much better to be healthy. I have also learned it is much easier to have faith not to get sick than it is to have faith for healing when you are already sick.

There is a further benefit to the power of the Holy Spirit in the body of the believer: *"So that your youth is renewed like the eagle's"* (Psalm 103:5). The resurrection life is more than equal to the ravages of sickness and disease, and it can even, in a certain measure, counterbalance the workings of old age. The Scripture says, *"Moses was one hundred and twenty years old when he died. His eyes were not dim nor his natural vigor* diminished" (Deuteronomy 34:7). Moses spent so much time in the presence of God that he really was living in a different kind of atmosphere than the other Israelites.

The environment we live in makes a significant difference. A woman told me she and her husband went home for the holidays and had a reunion with other members of the family who were not Spirit-baptized believers. They all arrived healthy but started talking about their sicknesses. After about three days of talking about their sicknesses, most of them were sick. She and her husband said, "We were just glad to get out of that atmosphere." The environment you live in has much to do with what you experience. I firmly believe the Spirit-filled believer should create an environment around him of positive faith, confidence, and praise.

An Atmosphere of Power that Heals

The Holy Spirit's power for healing indwelled Jesus from the time of His baptism in the river Jordan. There were instances when this power flowed through Him in an almost tangible way. One example of this was when the woman with the flow of blood came up behind Him in the crowd and touched the border of His garment.

Now a certain woman had a flow of blood for twelve years, and had suffered many things from many physicians. She had spent all that she had and was no better, but rather grew worse. When she heard about Jesus, she came behind Him in the crowd and touched His garment. For she said, "If only I may touch His clothes, I shall be made well." Immediately the fountain of her blood was dried up, and she felt in her body that she was healed of the affliction. And Jesus, immediately knowing in Himself that power had gone out of Him, turned around in the crowd and said, "Who touched My clothes?" (Mark 5:25–30)

Jesus felt healing power leave Him when the woman was healed. Let us look at another example: *"Now it happened on a certain day, as He was teaching, that there were Pharisees and teachers of the law sitting by, who had come out of every town of Galilee, Judea, and Jerusalem. And the power of the Lord was present to heal them"* (Luke 5:17). The whole atmosphere apparently was permeated with this healing power. In Luke 6:19, we find a situation similar to that of the woman with the flow of blood who was healed: *"And the whole multitude sought to touch Him, for power went out from Him and healed them all."* We will have experiences like that in our own lives and ministries when the spirit of healing or miracles will move into a meeting and almost everybody will be supernaturally touched by God. I have begun to see this on a small scale and I expect to see it increase.

The same supernatural healing power was associated with the ministry of Peter so that even his shadow brought healing:

They brought the sick out into the streets and laid them on beds and couches, that at least the shadow of Peter passing by might fall on some of them. Also a multitude gathered from the surrounding cities to Jerusalem, bringing sick people and those who were tormented by unclean spirits, and they were all healed. (Acts 5:15–16)

Such healings are not limited to the ministry of Jesus and the apostles. A brother in the Lord whom I knew was used in this way as he ministered in Argentina. He said at the height of the meetings he was conducting, he deliberately walked so his shadow fell on the sick, and they were healed. The meetings in Argentina shook the whole country from end to end in a way that all previous missionary efforts had absolutely been unable to achieve. This happened in the space of a few brief weeks. When God's power is liberated, we cannot measure what the results will be.

Specific Healings of Individuals

The examples in the last section were generally about mass healings occurring in an atmosphere of power. Let us now look at some scriptural accounts of the healing of individuals. We begin with the ministry of Jesus.

> *When the sun was setting, all those who had any that were sick with various diseases brought them to* [Jesus]*; and **He laid His hands on every one of them** and healed them.*
> (Luke 4:40, emphasis added)

Here we see that Jesus ministered to people individually. Each one whom He laid His hands on was healed. We see from this example that God does not always work healing in the same way. Sometimes, people could just touch Jesus and be healed, and other times He had to lay His hands on them individually.

We see this individual approach in the account of the healing of the leper.

> *When* [Jesus] *had come down from the mountain, great multitudes followed Him. And behold, a leper came and worshiped Him, saying, "Lord, if You are willing, You can make me clean." Then Jesus put out His hand and touched*

him, saying, "I am willing; be cleansed." Immediately his
leprosy was cleansed. (Matthew 8:1–3)

This visible healing of leprosy could really be considered a miracle. Jesus touched him, and he was immediately cured. Of course, one reason Jesus touched him was that people did not usually touch lepers. He could have healed him with some other method, but He went out of His way to touch the man to show him compassion.

Sometimes, the methods Jesus used in healing were distinctly unconventional. This shows we must rely totally on the leading of the Holy Spirit in healing. Let us look at two examples of unconventional healings in which people were healed after Jesus touched them. The first involves a man who was deaf:

Then they brought to Him one who was deaf and had an impediment in his speech, and they begged Him to put His hand on him. And He took him aside from the multitude, and put His fingers in his ears, and He spat and touched his tongue. Then, looking up to heaven, He sighed, and said to him, "Ephphatha," that is, "Be opened." Immediately his ears were opened, and the impediment of his tongue was loosed, and he spoke plainly. (Mark 7:32–35)

Then we have another remarkable account involving the healing of a blind man. *"Then He came to Bethsaida; and they brought a blind man to Him, and begged Him to touch him. So He took the blind man by the hand and led him out of the town"* (Mark 8:22–23). Why did Jesus lead the man out of town? There was probably such an atmosphere of unbelief there that the man could never have had the faith to be healed.

The passage continues, *"And when [Jesus] had spit on his eyes and put His hands on him, He asked him if he saw anything. And he looked up and said, 'I see men like trees, walking'"* (vv. 23–24). The man could see, but not clearly. Some people say all Jesus' healings were instantaneously complete. Yet Jesus depended, in a measure, on the response of faith in the person He was dealing with. *"Then He put His hands on his eyes again and made him look up. And he was restored and saw every-one clearly. Then He sent him away to his house, saying, 'Neither go into the town, nor tell anyone in the town'"* (vv. 25–26).

We must rely totally on the leading of the Holy Spirit in healing.

Apparently, Jesus just could not stand the atmosphere of that town. There was such an environment of unbelief there. Perhaps it was the man's relatives who were the problem. Sometimes, the hardest people to have faith in front of are your relatives. If all your relatives are unbelievers, you may have to have faith somewhere else. This man could not be healed in that particular town. And even when he was healed, he evidently could not keep his healing if he went back there.

Individual healings were also worked through the ministry of the early church. In the book of Acts, Paul and others were shipwrecked on the island of Malta after a terrible storm. When they came ashore, the islanders received them and opened up their homes to them. And there was one strategic healing God used to gain the attention of the whole island.

In that region there was an estate of the leading citizen of the island, whose name was Publius, who received us and

*entertained us courteously for three days. And it happened
that the father of Publius lay sick of a fever and dysentery.
Paul went in to him and prayed, and he laid his hands on him
and healed him. So when this was done, the rest of those on
the island who had diseases also came and were healed.*

(Acts 28:7–9)

Note the passage says Paul healed him. Of course, we
cannot heal anybody apart from Jesus and the power of the
Holy Spirit, but there are times when we can be so identified
with Him that we can heal people. Jesus said, *"He who believes in
Me, the works that I do he will do also"* (John 14:12). When Jesus
sent out the twelve disciples and then the seventy disciples to
minister in surrounding towns and cities, He told them, *"Heal
the sick."* (See, for example, Luke 10:9.) The Bible puts much
more responsibility on believers than most of us are willing to
recognize.

RESULTS OF GIFTS OF HEALINGS

We have seen that *gifts of healings* supernaturally restore
people to physical wholeness. When such a restoration comes,
it is a gift given through the person by whom the gift is manifested. Gifts of healings may be effected through the resurrection power of the Holy Spirit. They can be manifested in
an atmosphere for healing in which many are made whole, as
well in the healing of specific individuals under the guidance
of the Holy Spirit. Gifts of healings also result in creating an
atmosphere of belief for additional healing and an openness
to the gospel of Jesus Christ.

CHAPTER 9

WORKINGS OF Miracles

THE NATURE OF WORKINGS OF MIRACLES

I n 1 Corinthians 12:10, we read, *"To another* [is given] *the working of miracles."* As with gifts of healings, this gift is operated only under God's control. No one can work a miracle simply by an exercise of his own will.

As I said earlier, this gift is more properly designated as the double plural "workings of miracles." Moreover, Paul wrote about workings of miracles three times—in the tenth and twenty-eighth verses of 1 Corinthians 12 and in the fifth verse of Galatians 3. The Greek word translated *"miracles"* in these verses is the plural form of *dunamis. Dunamis* means "power," and therefore, translated literally, the gift would be "workings of powers." These workings refer to the God-given ability to demonstrate the supernatural power of the Holy Spirit at work. Each miracle is a working—a specific, definite manifestation of the gift.

GENERAL REFERENCES TO MIRACLES IN SCRIPTURE

A thread runs through the Scriptures wherever the word *dunamis* is used in the plural. Let us begin by looking at instances in the New Testament where *dunamis* is used in a general way for the miraculous, without a particular miraculous act being mentioned.

In Matthew 13:54, the people of Nazareth commented about Jesus when He first began His ministry: *"And when He had come to His own country, He taught them in their synagogue, so that they were astonished and said, 'Where did this Man get this wisdom and these mighty works?'"* The word *dunamis* in this case is translated *"mighty works."* Other Bible versions use *"miraculous powers."* The people were amazed at Jesus' wisdom and miracles and said, in effect, "Where did they come from? We know Him. He is just a carpenter's son. How is He able to do these things?" (See verses 55–56.)

Jesus' life and ministry were confirmed by miracles, signs, and wonders.

In Acts 2:22, Peter referred to Jesus in this way: *"Men of Israel, hear these words: Jesus of Nazareth, a Man attested by God to you by miracles [dunamis, powers], wonders, and signs which God did through Him in your midst, as you yourselves also know...."* God Almighty bore supernatural testimony to the life and ministry of Jesus by three things: miracles, wonders, and signs. Jesus was *"attested by God."* This fact was important for Peter's Jewish audience to understand. *"For Jews request a sign,"* Paul wrote, *"and Greeks seek after wisdom"* (1 Corinthians 1:22). Jews will never acknowledge a prophet who does not have a supernatural sign. It is ingrained in them. Their whole religious background is of men who came with a message from God and could prove it.

We really will never reach people as we should until we have supernatural evidence that what we are telling them is attested by God. I have been a missionary in two countries, and I would not step outside my own country to preach the gospel if I were not convinced God would bear supernatural testimony to the message He gives me. Otherwise, we would do better to stay at home and send literature. It will do the job much better unless we have something more than just words to offer people. That is the power of workings of miracles.

In speaking of his own apostleship, Paul wrote, *"Truly the signs of an apostle were accomplished among you with all perseverance, in signs and wonders and mighty deeds [dunamis]"* (2 Corinthians 12:12). The word translated *"mighty deeds"* is rendered *"miracles"* in other Bible versions. Once more, Paul made it clear that an apostle has to demonstrate his apostleship. He has to have supernatural attestation. Accompanying the signs of an apostle is a character quality, perseverance—the ability not to get discouraged or give up. Note that the same three words of attestation are used here that were used of Jesus in Acts 2:22: signs, wonders, and mighty deeds or miracles.

Another instance of *dunamis* is in Paul's epistle to the Galatians. In this letter, he was dealing with the fact that the believers, having known salvation by the grace and power of God, having experienced the baptism in the Holy Spirit, and having seen the miraculous, were now going back under the law of Moses and observing legal requirements through the influence of Judaizing teachers. It is very interesting that Paul was much more upset with the Galatians than he was with the Corinthians. The Corinthians had problems with all sorts of carnal sins, but Paul took time at the beginning of his first letter to thank God for the grace of God revealed to them. In his letter to the Galatians, he did not have any time to thank God for them. He said, *"I marvel that you are turning away so soon from Him who called you in the grace of Christ, to a different gospel"* (Galatians 1:6). Paul appeared to have been much more disturbed by the legalism than he was by the immorality, though he carefully corrected both errors. But legalism is a much greater danger to most Christians.

Note what Paul wrote in his rebuke to the Galatians:

> *This only I want to learn from you: Did you receive the Spirit by the works of the law, or by the hearing of faith? Are you so foolish? Having begun in the Spirit, are you now being made perfect by the flesh? Have you suffered so many things in vain; if indeed it was in vain? Therefore He who supplies the Spirit to you and works miracles [dunamis] among you, does He do it by the works of the law, or by the hearing of faith?* (Galatians 3:2–5)

The apostle was saying, "Did you receive the Holy Spirit as a result of being circumcised and keeping the law of Moses? No. You received the Holy Spirit when you believed the preaching of the gospel, somebody prayed and laid hands on you, and you began to speak with tongues. Are you going back to fleshly ordinances and rules after you have known what it is to taste the power and liberty of the Holy Spirit?"

Workings of miracles come by "the hearing of faith."

"*Supplies the Spirit to you*" (v. 5) refers to bringing people into the baptism in the Holy Spirit. This does not happen by being circumcised or being under the law of Moses but by faith, just as salvation comes by faith. Paul therefore put workings of miracles in the same category as receiving the Holy Spirit. They come by the hearing of faith. You listen to somebody expound the Word of God, and then by a simple act, you release your faith and it happens. It doesn't require a lot of agonizing or shouting; it isn't emotionalism. It is just hearing the Word of God with faith.

Another example of miracles mentioned in a general way in the Scriptures is in Hebrews:

How shall we escape if we neglect so great a salvation, which at the first began to be spoken by the Lord, and was confirmed to us by those who heard Him, God also bearing witness both with signs and wonders, with various miracles [dunamis], and gifts of the Holy Spirit, according to His own will? (Hebrews 2:3–4)

Four manifestations of God's power are mentioned here: signs, wonders, various miracles, and gifts of the Holy Spirit. *"Gifts"* in this verse would be better translated as "distributions." The testimony of God to the gospel message was supernatural through and through. It should be just the same today.

MIRACLES AND DELIVERANCE

Before we discuss specific miracles, I want to point out the relationship between gifts of miracles and the casting out of evil spirits. In almost every place where the word *dunamis* is used, there is a reference to casting out demons. For example, in Mark we read,

Now John answered Him, saying, "Teacher, we saw someone who does not follow us [who is not in our group] casting out demons in Your name, and we forbade him because he does not follow us." But Jesus said, "Do not forbid him,

for no one who works a miracle [dunamis] in My name can
soon afterward speak evil of Me."   (Mark 9:38–39)

Notice Jesus referred to the casting out of evil spirits in His name as doing a miracle.

We find a similar situation in the description of the ministry of Philip in Samaria.

And the multitudes with one accord heeded the things spoken by Philip, hearing and seeing the miracles [a different Greek word] *which he did. For unclean spirits, crying with a loud voice, came out of many who were possessed; and many who were paralyzed and lame were healed....Then Simon himself also believed; and when he was baptized he continued with Philip, and was amazed, seeing the miracles [dunamis] and signs which were done.*   (Acts 8:6–7, 13)

The correct translation from the Greek is "seeing the signs and *great* miracles that were done." The great miracles Simon saw were not just the paralyzed and the lame being visibly healed, but also evil spirits coming out of people in a manifest way. I have found similar results in my ministry. The Lord revealed to us that if we would continue to cast out evil spirits, miraculous healings would follow. And I have seen the lame and paralyzed healed. It is remarkable how accurate the Scripture is. If we press on, there is more ahead. The best is yet to be.

Another example of the connection between miracles and deliverance is found in Acts 19. *"God worked unusual [*"special"* KJV] miracles [dunamis] by the hands of Paul, so that even handkerchiefs or aprons were brought from his body to the sick, and the diseases left them and the evil spirits went out of them"* (vv. 11–12).

The word *"unusual"* or *"special"* tells us miracles were normal in the early church, but that here was something even outside the norm.

In Scripture passages where an actual miracle or miracles is specified, therefore, there is generally a reference to evil spirits going out. This is one of the manifest demonstrations of the power of God.

MANIFESTATIONS OF SPECIFIC MIRACLES

Water into Wine

Let us now look at some examples of specific miracles recorded in the New Testament. Jesus' very first miracle was turning water into wine.

> *There was a wedding in Cana of Galilee, and the mother of Jesus was there. Now both Jesus and His disciples were invited to the wedding. And when they ran out of wine, the mother of Jesus said to Him, "They have no wine." Jesus said to her, "Woman, what does your concern have to do with Me? My hour has not yet come." His mother said to the servants, "Whatever He says to you, do it." Now there were set there six waterpots of stone, according to the manner of purification of the Jews, containing twenty or thirty gallons apiece. Jesus said to them, "Fill the waterpots with water." And they filled them up to the brim. And He said to them, "Draw some out now, and take it to the master of the feast." And they took it.* (John 2:1–8)

Jesus told the servants to *fill* the six pots with water—that's faith. Then He said to draw some out and give it to the master of the feast. Somewhere between the time they drew it out and the time it got to the master of the feast, it had changed into wine. That was a miracle. (See John 2:9–11.) You might call it a sign or you might call it a wonder, but it fits in that category.

Feeding the Five Thousand

Another miracle was Jesus multiplying the loaves and fish to feed thousands of people.

> Jesus lifted up His eyes, and seeing a great multitude coming toward Him, He said to Philip, "Where shall we buy bread, that these may eat?" But this He said to test him, for He Himself knew what He would do. Philip answered Him, "Two hundred denarii worth of bread is not sufficient for them, that every one of them may have a little." One of His disciples, Andrew, Simon Peter's brother, said to Him, "There is a lad here who has five barley loaves and two small fish, but what are they among so many?" Then Jesus said, "Make the people sit down." Now there was much grass in the place. So the men sat down, in number about five thousand. And Jesus took the loaves, and when He had given thanks He distributed them to the disciples, and the disciples to those sitting down; and likewise of the fish, as much as they wanted. So when they were filled, He said to His disciples, "Gather up the fragments that remain, so that nothing is lost." Therefore they gathered them up, and filled twelve baskets with the fragments of the five barley loaves which were left over by those who had eaten. Then those men, when they had seen the sign that Jesus did, said, "This is truly the Prophet who is to come into the world."
>
> (John 6:5–14)

Jesus wanted to feed five thousand men, not including women and children, and He had five loaves and two fish.

What did He do? One very simple thing. He gave thanks to the Lord and then started to give out the food. It fed everyone, with some left over. Do you know how much food was gathered up at the end? The passage says it filled twelve baskets. Another time, Jesus fed four thousand people with seven loaves and a few fish. In this case, there were seven basketsful left over, but a different word is used for basket the second time because these were much larger baskets. Not only were the people fed, but also the leftovers were abundant. (See, for example, Mark 8:1–9.)

Jesus required submission to His authority before He fed the people.

Notice Jesus conducted this miracle in a very orderly and systematic way. In the Mark 6 account of the feeding of the five thousand, we read Jesus told the disciples to have people sit down in groups, and they sat down on the grass in groups of fifty and a hundred. Jesus required order and submission to His authority before He fed the people. The same is true for us in a spiritual sense. Some people do not want to be joined to anybody or be under the authority of anybody else. Because of this, they are not able to be spiritually fed.

A Creative Miracle for a Man Blind from Birth

Then we have the remarkable case of Jesus healing a man who had been born blind.

Now as Jesus passed by, He saw a man who was blind from birth. And His disciples asked Him, saying, "Rabbi, who sinned, this man or his parents, that he was born blind?" Jesus answered, "Neither this man nor his parents sinned,

but that the works of God should be revealed in him...."
When He had said these things, He spat on the ground and
made clay with the saliva; and He anointed the eyes of the
blind man with the clay. And He said to him, "Go, wash in
the pool of Siloam" (which is translated, Sent). So he went
and washed, and came back seeing.   (John 9:1–3, 6–7)

Jesus anointed the eyes of a blind man with clay and told him to wash in the pool at Siloam. He went, washed, and was able to see. It was not the clay itself that healed the man; yet, when he obeyed Jesus' instructions by an act of faith and washed in the pool, the Holy Spirit responded to his obedience and accomplished what no human being could do. The power of the Holy Spirit turned that clay into eyes. I believe Jesus put the clay on the man's eyes just to advertise that He was the Creator and that any time, in the will of the Father, He could make clay into flesh. According to Genesis 2:7, the Lord God formed man from the clay of the ground and then breathed into his nostrils the breath of life, the divine Spirit of God, and man became a living being with a spirit, soul, and body. This was therefore an outstanding miracle, a vindication of the fact that Jesus was the eternal Creator who had come to live among humanity.

The Healing of a Man Lame from Birth

In the ministry of the apostles, there was the healing miracle of the man who was born lame and had never walked.

And a certain man lame from his mother's womb was car-
ried, whom they laid daily at the gate of the temple which
is called Beautiful, to ask alms from those who entered the
temple; who, seeing Peter and John about to go into the

temple, asked for alms. And fixing his eyes on him, with John, Peter said, "Look at us." So he gave them his attention, expecting to receive something from them. Then Peter said, "Silver and gold I do not have, but what I do have I give you: In the name of Jesus Christ of Nazareth, rise up and walk." And he took him by the right hand and lifted him up, and immediately his feet and ankle bones received strength. So he, leaping up, stood and walked and entered the temple with them; walking, leaping, and praising God.

(Acts 3:2–8)

This man was sitting at the Beautiful Gate of the temple when he saw Peter and John coming. He stretched out his hand expecting to receive money, when Peter said, *"Silver and gold I do not have, but what I do have I give you."* Obviously, you cannot give something if you do not have it. The trouble with so many of us is that we do not have much spiritually to give other people. But Peter said, in effect, "I don't have silver and I don't have gold, but in the name of Jesus, rise up and walk."

While the man was still sitting there, Peter stretched out his hand and lifted him up. When the man began to rise up, he was healed. It is most important to see that people very rarely receive anything by just sitting passively. You have to do something to exercise your faith. Faith without works, without corresponding acts, is dead. (See James 2:20, 26.) I have learned the crucial point in a miracle is getting a person to do a small act that starts his faith moving. In many cases, it does not matter much what it is, but the moment people begin to act, things begin to happen. As Peter started to lift the man up, and as the man responded, in that moment of acting, the supernatural power of God straightened out his ankles and legs.

I have personally witnessed many legs straightened. I have seen people with bowlegs have their legs visibly come together. In addition, a friend of mine was asked to pray for a high school teacher who was crippled with arthritis and clubfeet. He prayed for him and commanded him to rise up and walk, and he did so. The next day, instead of appearing in a wheelchair, he walked into his classroom. My friend said that convinced those students more than a hundred sermons could have that God is alive. We have an obligation to our generation to demonstrate God is truly alive. I have seen bumper stickers that say, "My God is not dead." That is fine, but let us see a demonstration. This is what the world is looking for. When they see it, it is amazing who will respond. The most hard-hearted and cynical can become the most enthusiastic.

> We have an obligation to our generation to demonstrate God is truly alive.

The Raising of Eutychus from the Dead

The apostle Paul was involved in the miracle of raising a man named Eutychus from the dead.

Now on the first day of the week, when the disciples came together to break bread, Paul, ready to depart the next day, spoke to them and continued his message until midnight. There were many lamps in the upper room where they were gathered together. And in a window sat a certain young man named Eutychus, who was sinking into a deep sleep. He was overcome by sleep; and as Paul continued speaking, he fell down from the third story and was taken up dead.

But Paul went down, fell on him, and embracing him said, "Do not trouble yourselves, for his life is in him."…And they brought the young man in alive, and they were not a little comforted. (Acts 20:7–10, 12)

Some people would have been thrown off balance if that had happened in the middle of their giving a sermon, yet Paul almost took it in stride. Through Paul, the power of the Holy Spirit worked the miracle of bringing Eutychus back to life.

MIRACLES AND ACTS OF FAITH

If you study the miracles in Scripture, you will find that almost every time, an act of faith triggered them. Sometimes, it was a very simple act. For example, when Moses and the Israelites arrived at Marah, the waters were bitter, and they could not drink from them. Moses cried to the Lord, and the Lord showed him a tree. When he threw the tree into the water, the waters became sweet. (See Exodus 15:23–25). The tree itself did not sweeten the water; it was the power of God. Yet Moses had to throw the tree in. He did not slip the tree in quietly; he *threw* it in with a splash. In other words, he committed himself. Faith is not an experiment; it is a commitment.

Jesus Himself did some seemingly strange things while doing miracles, such as putting clay in a blind man's eyes and spitting and touching a deaf man's tongue. He also told other people to do things that were absurd in the natural, such as going and washing in a specific pool. But those simple acts liberated the healing power of God.

MIRACLES AND HEALINGS

In one way, healings merge with miracles; an instantaneous, visible healing is a miracle. In another way, miracles merge with faith. But of the gifts of power, the ministry of miracles is put before the ministry of healings, according to 1 Corinthians 12:28: *"And God has appointed these in the church: first apostles, second prophets, third teachers, after that miracles, then gifts of healings...."* Earlier, we read that when Jesus went to His hometown of Nazareth, the people would not accept Him because of their unbelief. *"He could do no mighty work there, except that He laid His hands on a few sick people and healed them"* (Mark 6:5). Again, in the Greek, the term translated as *"mighty work"* is *dunamis,* the same word for miracle we have been looking at. Jesus could not do a miracle in Nazareth, but He could do a little healing. Apparently, a miracle is on a slightly higher level than a healing.

There is not any more obvious need in the church today than for the exercise of gifts of miracles because this is what the world needs to see as a demonstration of the presence and power of God. We should be praying that God will fully restore this gift to His people.

PART 4

THE VOCAL *Gifts*

CHAPTER 10

KINDS OF Tongues AND INTERPRETATION OF Tongues

Now we come to the third group of spiritual gifts: the vocal gifts. These derive their name from the fact that they necessarily operate through human vocal cords. Under the vocal gifts, we have different kinds of tongues, interpretation of tongues, and prophecy.

THE VOCAL GIFTS

Let us begin with some basic definitions of these gifts. These definitions are not intended to be all-encompassing, but rather practical introductions. Note that the words *to speak* are central to each one.

Kinds of tongues is the ability given by the Holy Spirit to speak in a language not understood by the speaker.

Interpretation of tongues is the ability given by the Holy Spirit to speak, in a language understood by the speaker, the meaning of words previously spoken in an unknown language.

Prophecy is the ability to speak words given by the Holy Spirit in a language understood by the speaker.

We have said that the previous two groups of gifts—the gifts of revelation and the gifts of power—remain under the control of God. No one by an act of his will can operate a gift of healing or a working of miracles, or have a word of wisdom or a word of knowledge. This doesn't mean the human will does not play any part in the exercise of these gifts, because if the human will does not yield to the Holy Spirit, the gifts cannot operate. However, the initiative in those six gifts remains with God.

Yet when we come to the vocal gifts, there is no question that, in some measure—it varies with different people—they are placed under human control. Speaking from personal experience, I can speak in an unknown tongue at will at any time of the day or night, without any reservation that I know of. I can also interpret very frequently. I do not know how often I might prophesy, but I know that if I sought to, I could prophesy at any meeting. God gave me that ability many years ago and I have never lost it.

If you do not yield to the Holy Spirit, the gifts cannot operate in your life.

On the other hand, I do not just prophesy at any meeting. I learned quickly that, while these gifts are placed under our control, we are also responsible for what we do with them. One of the first things we have to do in the field of the vocal gifts is learn from the Word of God the purposes for which they are given, the right way to use them, and the ways we should not use them.

In 1 Corinthians 14, Paul gave many instructions regarding how and when to exercise the gifts and how and when not to. For instance, Paul said that, normally, in a meeting, two or three people are to speak in tongues, and no more. Obviously, more might have the ability to do so, but they are to restrain themselves for purposes of order. Similarly, only two or three prophets may speak at a meeting. If someone wants to speak out loud in an unknown tongue, there must be an interpreter (either the person who gave the tongue or another person) or else the tongue should not be spoken.

It is clear from the examples Paul gave that people retain the power to either exercise or not exercise these gifts. There is no way to calculate the number of mistakes and disasters that have arisen from people not understanding they are responsible to learn to control the vocal gifts of the Spirit.

KINDS OF TONGUES

Paul wrote, *"To another* [is given] *different kinds of tongues"* (1 Corinthians 12:10). This verse does not refer to the gift of speaking in an unknown tongue that is given to all believers at the baptism in the Holy Spirit. Concerning this gift, Paul wrote, *"He who speaks in a tongue does not speak to men but to God, for no one understands him; however, in the spirit he speaks mysteries"* (1 Corinthians 14:2). Every believer may exercise this form of tongues in private communion with God. He speaks *"mysteries,"* or things not understood by the mind, for the purpose of edification in his personal spiritual life. In contrast, the gift of kinds of tongues is plural in both its aspects, and it is set in the public assembly for ministry to that assembly. These tongues are not for personal edification but for the building up of the body of Christ in a local church.

PUBLIC VERSUS PRIVATE TONGUES

To give us a broader perspective of this public gift of tongues, let us look at 1 Corinthians 12:28, where Paul listed different ministries given by God for the public assembly. *"And God has appointed these in the church: first apostles, second prophets, third teachers, after that miracles, then gifts of healings, helps, administrations, varieties* [kinds] *of tongues."* When Paul talked about the church in this verse, he was not speaking of the church universal but was specifically referring to a public assembly of God's people who have come together to minister to one another through the operation of the gifts.

In the above verse, the gifts are listed, more or less, in order of seniority. We noted this fact in the chapter on workings of miracles, in which we saw that miracles are put on a somewhat higher level than healings. This type of ordering is unusual, however. In most places, Paul did not list a hierarchy of gifts. For example, there is nothing to suggest he was listing the most important gifts first in 1 Corinthians 12:8–10, when he listed the spiritual gifts we are examining in this book.

The public gift of tongues is for the edification of an assembly of believers.

In fact, Paul wrote various passages that might suggest the most highly prized gift is prophecy, which is listed quite near the end of that list. Yet here we have a definite order. *"**First** apostles, **second** prophets, **third** teachers, **after that** miracles, **then** gifts of healings...."* The first five, at least, are listed apparently in order of seniority.

The ministry of the Word takes precedence over all other forms of ministry because it has the final authority. This is why those who have the ministry of the Word are listed first. The ministries of the Word are followed by the supernatural ministries that come by the exercise of the gifts of miracles and healings. Then we have helps and administrations or "steering," which means indicating the way the meeting or a group should go. Finally, we have varieties of tongues.

In the Greek, exactly the same phrase is used in 1 Corinthians 12:28 for varieties of tongues that is used in 1 Corinthians 12:10 for different kinds of tongues. I therefore prefer to translate verse twenty-eight as different kinds of tongues also. Incidentally, the Greek word we translate as *"kinds"* is the same word from which the English word *genus* is derived. So what we are talking about in this gift are different genuses of tongues or different genres of tongues.

It is clear from the context of 1 Corinthians 12 we are not dealing with a tongue used in personal communion with God. As I wrote earlier, that is a private gift, while this is a public gift. If we do not clearly understand the difference, we will not be able to comprehend the context of what Paul said concerning the different aspects of these tongues. The purpose of different kinds of tongues is public ministry in the assembly, just as apostles, prophets, teachers, miracles, gifts of healings, helps, and administrations have that purpose. We must completely distinguish in our minds kinds of tongues from the private use of a tongue.

Following his list of gifts in 1 Corinthians 12:28, Paul clearly implied not all believers have a ministry of tongues in the public assembly. He wrote, *"Are all apostles? Are all prophets? Are all teachers? Are all workers of miracles? Do all have gifts of healings? Do all speak with tongues? Do all interpret?"* (vv. 29–30). Paul asked these rhetorical questions, and I think everybody would agree the way the questions are asked implies the answer in each case is no.

Some people deduce from these verses that, because not all have the gift of tongues, tongues are not a necessarily result of the baptism in the Holy Spirit. Yet the question Paul was asking is, "In the *public assembly*, do all have the operation of kinds of tongues?" The answer is no. I know many people who are baptized in the Spirit and are able to communicate regularly with God privately in an unknown tongue who do not have a ministry of tongues in the public assembly. So Paul was not talking about the result of the baptism in the Holy Spirit. He was talking about different types of ministries in a public gathering of believers.

DIFFERENT KINDS OF TONGUES FOR PUBLIC ASSEMBLY

I now offer you my understanding of what Paul meant by kinds of tongues. I have arrived at this conclusion from years of study, meditation, and prayer, as well as on the basis of observation and experience in a number of different groups in many different countries. However, I have to say it still remains my opinion, and that others might feel differently.

Different kinds of tongues can include praise, intercession, rebuke, and exhortation.

I do not believe it means different languages as, for instance, sometimes Russian, sometimes Greek, sometimes French, sometimes Sanskrit, and so on. I was in New Zealand teaching on the work of the Holy Spirit, and I had come to the place in my series of messages where I was about to teach on kinds of tongues. I had already seen the fact that both parts of this gift are plural and had come to the conclusion that it did not refer to different languages. One morning I woke up with this phrase in my mind, as clear and distinct as anything: "Kinds of tongues: praise, intercession, rebuke, and exhortation." I feel the Holy Spirit was showing me at least a part of the meaning of kinds of tongues—different kinds of prayer given in tongues that suit the types of prayer. It also refers to exhortation or instruction. I am in no way suggesting these four types exhaust the possibilities.

I mentioned that the word *kinds* in kinds of tongues is related to the English word *genus*. Therefore, the various kinds of languages are distinguished on the basis of the *use* or *purpose* for which they are given. As background, let us look at two passages from 1 Timothy. Paul wrote,

> *I hope to come to you shortly; but if I am delayed, I write so that you may know how you ought to conduct yourself in the house of God, which is the church of the living God, the pillar and ground of the truth.*   (1 Timothy 3:14–15)

We see that the primary purpose for which 1 Timothy was written was to instruct Timothy in correct behavior in the local church. With this in mind, we can note a very important point of emphasis in regard to kinds of prayer, which Paul wrote to Timothy earlier in his letter:

> *Therefore I exhort first of all that supplications, prayers, intercessions, and giving of thanks be made for all men.*
> (1 Timothy 2:1)

In other words, the primary ministry of the local congregation is prayer. If we do not see this, we will fail to understand many other biblical truths, and we will not be able to enter into the full experience of what God has for us. If we bypass prayer, we will not obtain the results the New Testament speaks about, for prayer is the generator that produces the power that operates the other aspects of life in the assembly.

For example, if you skip prayer and immediately implement a program in the church, you will find you do not have the power to operate it. It is like having a building wired for electricity with light, heat, and sound fixtures but lacking a connection to a generator. Nothing works because there is no power. This is how I understand the place of prayer in the local assembly.

The whole subject of prayer and tongues is such a full one it always grieves me to hear people refer to tongues as if they were small and insignificant. It is a tremendous subject that reaches into many different aspects of Christian living. After studying and meditating on it for decades, I have not come anywhere near to the depth of it.

In many ways, although the gift of kinds of tongues is one of the hardest to understand and enter into, it is also one of fullest and most effective when it is correctly operated.

FOUR KINDS OF TONGUES

Let us now relate different kinds of tongues to different kinds of praying. Again, I am not suggesting these are the only kinds of prayer in relation to tongues in the public assembly, but they are important aspects of it.

PRAISE

Although we are talking about the exercise of kinds of tongues in a public assembly, the size of the assembly does not need to be very large. The smallest assembly is two or three believers gathered together in the name of Jesus. (See Matthew 18:20.) Many times, a very small group really committed to the Lord in prayer and ready to do business with God—instead of being out to play spiritual games or get spiritual thrills—is one of the most effective prayer groups. Sometimes, when a prayer group becomes larger, the motives of some of the people in it can be questionable and there is not the same unity, power, and spiritual impact. While people always seem to want their prayer groups to grow bigger, the number of people does not really matter; it is the degree of unity and purpose that makes prayer effective.

If we minister to the Lord, He will minister to our needs in His timing.

Suppose, therefore, we have a group of two, fifteen, fifty, or five hundred people who are in the presence of the Lord, ministering to Him. This concept of ministering to the Lord is an important one. Many Christians' idea of prayer is simply to come together with a list of things they want God to do. Yet experience shows that if we minister to the Lord, then, in His timing, He will minister very rapidly to our needs. We do not usually need to do a lot of begging and pleading with God.

Within a group such as I just described, whether it is small or large, somebody may be given a tongue of praise. When you hear it, you recognize that a human spirit is adoring, exalting, and worshipping the Creator. This can be a thrilling experience. And the result is that it liberates the rest of the group. They all begin to join together in exalting God. The purpose of this tongue of praise is to lead the whole group into worship and praise. It fulfills its purpose without any need for interpretation—though sometimes an interpretation of a tongue that is purely praise and worship does come, and it can be very beautiful.

INTERCESSION

Let us consider another situation under the genre of intercession. A group may be praying about a person or a situation, but they cannot seem to pray through to victory. Or, they may not know which way to pray or which way the meeting should go. In such cases, God the Holy Spirit may give someone an intercessory tongue. This may be the specific prayer that person or situation needs, or it may be a prayer for the group as a whole to be directed rightly and know the will of the Lord.

I have noticed that, quite often after what I would call an intercessory tongue, there will be an utterance in prophecy. Yet the two are not directly connected, as tongues and interpretation are. Rather, the tongue of intercession liberated the prophecy that God wanted to be brought forth. I have seen this happen many times. We learn to distinguish between tongues and interpretation, and tongues followed by prophecy.

REBUKE

Another type of public tongue that people sometimes find rather surprising and even upsetting is tongues in the form of rebuke. We read several times in the gospels that Jesus rebuked situations. He stood over Peter's mother-in-law and rebuked the fever. (See Luke 4:38–39.) You don't rebuke something that is purely a physical condition. If you rebuke something, there is a person or personality behind it, which implies an evil spirit may have been involved. Earlier, we saw that when Jesus and the disciples were crossing the sea of Galilee and the storm was about to sink their ship, Jesus stood up and rebuked the wind and the waves. (See Mark 4:35–41.) Remember that the literal meaning in the Greek for *"be still"* (v. 39) is "be muzzled." He was dealing with a personality behind the situation.

The Holy Spirit within Christians will sometimes do the same. When we begin to pray for a particular physical or mental need, for example, the Holy Spirit will seem to rise up within someone, even in anger. I have seen this many times. It comes out in a torrent like a dam bursting and a river sweeping down, carrying away the boulders and debris before it. This is the Holy Spirit turned loose against the presence and operation of the devil in some form or another. People who are not familiar with this manifestation become scared and ask how the Holy Spirit could sound like that. We have to learn the Holy Spirit has the infinite wisdom of God, and He sees behind the situation we are praying about, so that He will turn His power loose against the devil for that situation.

The Holy Spirit has the infinite wisdom of God to see behind the situation.

My wife Lydia prayed for the sick many times in this way, and it came out like a roar. To me, what matters is that the person was healed. For example, we were in a meeting in Ohio that was rather quiet because the people were not very free in the Spirit. A man asked, "Would you pray for me? I have arthritis." My wife and I stood behind him, and Lydia laid her hands on his back. Suddenly, she gave a very loud, fierce roar. The man went up in the air about two inches and came down. He said, "My, you frightened me! But my arthritis is gone."

This was an example of tongues for rebuke. There was no need for any interpretation; it would have been out of place to give an interpretation. Sometimes, this type of tongues can be somewhat embarrassing. Yet if you shut off the embarrassment, you also shut off the gift. I know one man who had this gift, and people he ministered to would fall down in the Spirit by the dozens and hundreds. I have seen two hundred people in Africa on their backs at one time as he ministered. He told me one day, "I asked God if I could do it without people going on their backs because it provokes so much criticism and opposition. The people didn't go on their backs after that, but they didn't get healed either." After a while he prayed, "God, You heal the people whatever way You want to do it." We are not to dictate terms to the Holy Spirit. All we have to do is yield ourselves and cooperate with Him.

EXHORTATION

A fourth kind of tongue in the public assembly is exhortation, where the Holy Spirit speaks a specific word to the group of believers gathered. Obviously, since it is given in a tongue, its purpose will not be fulfilled unless it is followed by interpretation in the language understood by the group.

THE INTERPRETATION OF TONGUES

Let us now look at the gift of interpretation of tongues, which we have defined as the ability given by the Holy Spirit to speak, in a language understood by the speaker, the meaning of words previously spoken in an unknown language. Again, it is obvious that interpretation has relevance only to a situation where an utterance has previously been given in an unknown tongue. If there has been no unknown tongue, there can never be any logical or reasonable use for an interpretation.

Paul wrote, *"I wish you all spoke with tongues, but even more that you prophesied; for he who prophesies is greater than he who speaks with tongues, **unless indeed he interprets**, that the church may receive edification"* (1 Corinthians 14:5, emphasis added). The apostle was saying that speaking in an unknown tongue, in itself, is not edifying to the church unless the tongue is followed by its interpretation. Apparently, in this case, a tongue of exhortation followed by interpretation is equivalent to prophecy. It accomplishes the same purpose and it must obviously be judged by the same standards. We see again that what Paul said in 1 Corinthians 14:2 about an unknown tongue communicating only with God does not apply to his statement in 1 Corinthians 14:5 about a tongue followed by interpretation in the public assembly. If it were a mystery that could not be understood, it could not be interpreted.

In the assembly, we should bless and minister to our fellow believers.

Paul said, *"I thank my God I speak with tongues more than you all; yet in the church I would rather speak five words with my understanding, that I may teach others also, than ten thousand words in a tongue"* (1 Corinthians 14:18–19). Some people who are critics of tongues know verse nineteen, but they have not read verse eighteen. They ask, "Didn't Paul say he would rather speak five words in a known tongue than ten thousand in an unknown tongue?" Yes, but he also said he thanked God he spoke with tongues more than all the rest of the Corinthian believers.

When you form a picture from Paul's letters of how much the Corinthian church spoke in tongues, it is obvious Paul spoke in tongues a great deal. It is equally obvious he did not normally do it in the public assembly. Where did Paul do all this speaking in tongues? Clearly, it was in his private communion with God. This shows us again the two types of tongues are quite distinct, for Paul essentially said it would be no good for him to stand up for an hour in the public assembly and speak in an unknown tongue. It would be out of place, since it would not edify or help anybody. But in the assembly, our aim is to communicate with our fellow believers, to bless and to minister to them, and we need to operate on that basis. We have to speak in a way that reaches them and that they can understand.

I have seen a situation many times where somebody will speak in an unknown tongue out loud, and it will not be followed by interpretation; it will not fulfill any function or ministry but will confuse, disturb, and perhaps frighten those who do not understand it. This is a misuse of an unknown tongue. Again, in the public assembly, the primary purpose to which everything else should be subjected is the edifying and blessing of our fellow believers. This is why the public ministry of tongues for exhortation must be followed by interpretation.

In 1 Corinthians 14:28, Paul said, *"If there is no interpreter, let him keep silent in church* [the public assembly], *and let him speak to himself and to God."* Suppose you feel you want to pray in an unknown tongue, but you are in the public assembly and realize it is not going to be interpreted. What do you do? It is very simple. You do it under your breath; you speak only to yourself and to God. I have known people who have been baptized in the Holy Spirit for years but who did not know they could pray quietly in tongues under their breath. Yet this is what Paul was saying in the above verse as a solution to the problem of a lack of interpretation.

The Nature of Interpretation

To properly exercise the gift of interpretation of tongues, we must understand its nature. Interpretation must not necessarily be understood to mean a word-for-word translation, but rather a rendering of the general sense of what was spoken in the tongue. Let me illustrate this by my own experiences of preaching through an interpreter in a foreign language.

By using an interpreter, I have learned to trim much extraneous preaching and eliminate a lot of wasted time. For instance, I have found it is no good trying to make jokes because they are usually impossible to translate. Likewise, I cannot use excessively slangy expressions because they get lost in translation. It is also useless to pile up a lot of bombastic words because they perplex the interpreter and get you nowhere. When you preach through an interpreter, all you can give is the meat; the frills have to fall away. The only thing that will get through to an interpreter is something that has real meaning and is helpful.

Let me give you another illustration. When I was in East Africa, my preaching in English was interpreted into Swahili, which is generally the common language there. I had two of the best interpreters in the country, but they were absolutely different. One would use at least twice as many words as the other. The first was rather blunt, brief, and to the point. Yet, in some ways, he got the message across better.

These experiences really brought home to me that interpreting is not exactly translating. It is conveying the meaning in a way that can be understood. So the interpretation of tongues may convey only the general meaning of the words.

However, it is also possible for interpretation to come in the form of a literal translation. I have witnessed occasions where a person has given an interpretation of a tongue spoken in a language he did not know, and this was verified by someone else who knew the language as an accurate word-for-word translation. These examples help to explain why an interpretation of tongues may be longer, shorter, or a similar length in regard to the length of the tongue itself.

Interpretation of tongues may not be word-for-word, but will convey the meaning.

In addition, my experience with interpreters has shown me each interpreter conveys his individual personality. I believe this also applies to those who exercise the gift of interpretation of tongues. If you listen to people exercising the gift of interpretation, you will find their own personalities are still perceptible as they operate in the gift. For example, I have been asked why some people give interpretations using King James English. My answer is that a person may have grown up with the King James Bible so that he has it in his heart, and therefore it will come out naturally as part of who he is. Another will give an interpretation in modern English. There are different kinds of interpreters, and the gift will operate according to their personalities.

THE *Gifts* OF THE SPIRIT

When I was in New Zealand, at the same time God taught me about the kinds of tongues for prayer, one of our worship meetings was broadcast during the main news program on one of the TV channels. The man who televised it was not a Christian, but he was extremely interested in speaking in tongues. I spoke on the topic of tongues and then we worshipped God and praised Him in tongues. They broadcast this for twenty minutes at peak news time. Friends told me afterward it was so popular they repeated it later that year as the most interesting newscast of that particular period. However, a group of Christians in the city listened and said, "You can see it wasn't real because even when Mr. Prince spoke in tongues, you could recognize his voice and his accent." They did not realize that operating in the gifts of the Spirit will not set aside a person's personality or the normal sound of his voice. This is why, when people give interpretations, each does so in his own particular style.

Compare the utterances of the Old Testament prophets. For example, look at the words of Amos, Hosea, and Isaiah, who were more or less contemporaries. You could not mistake an utterance of one for another. Yet they were all inspired by the Holy Spirit. The Holy Spirit loves and delights in human personality. He never makes a human being a rubber stamp; He never sets aside personality and uses a person like a robot or a machine. Yet an evil spirit will do that. That is a great difference between the Spirit of God and satanic spirits. God created human personality, and He esteems it, appreciates it, and cultivates it. But the devil overrides it and tramples upon it. This is one of the ways you can know whether something is of the Spirit of God or if another kind of spirit is at work. If it is a spirit that enslaves and sets aside the normal human personality, it cannot be God's Spirit.

The Operation of the Gift of Interpretation

We will next consider ways in which the gift of interpretation operates. To start with a general principle, 1 Corinthians 12:6 says, *"There are diversities of activities ["operations" KJV], but it is the same God who works all in all."* In other words, two men may have the same ministry, but it will operate in their lives very differently. Let us take two well-known examples. Two men who have the obvious ministry gift of an evangelist are Billy Graham and Oral Roberts. Yet there is a very definite, conspicuous difference between the ministry of one and the ministry of the other. Though the ministry is the same, there are diversities of operations. The same is true with the gifts. One person will have a gift of healing that operates in one way, while another person will have a gift of healing that operates completely differently.

Two men may have the same ministry, but it will operate in their lives very differently.

The following are diverse ways in which a person might receive interpretation. I have heard all these testified to by people at one time or another.

AN INTRODUCTORY PHRASE OR SENTENCE

In addition to the personality and stylistic differences we have noted, the gift of interpretation does not operate in exactly the same way through each person. In my experience, one person may initially be given an introductory phrase; then he must launch out in faith with the rest of it. This is what usually happens to me. When I receive interpretation, the first sentence will be given to me very clearly and forcefully in my mind. If I begin to speak the first sentence in faith, and with authority, the rest will follow. But if I hold back, nothing more comes. Suppose I were to say, "Lord, if You will give me the whole message, then I'll speak it. I'm not quite sure that anything else is going to come, and I'll look rather silly if I just speak out this sentence." I would never receive the whole message because you cannot set aside the principle of faith. Hebrews 11:6 tells us, *"Without faith it is impossible to please [God]."* Everything we do for God has to be done in faith.

Many people hold back and do not receive the interpretation they were meant to speak. I have talked to people who have said, "I think the Lord gave me the interpretation, but I only got one sentence." I have told them, "You will never get more until you start to use the one sentence you have." Similarly, some people say, "I believe I received the baptism in the Holy Spirit, but I only speak one word." I tell them to go on speaking that word, to be thankful for what they have, and God will give them more. Using what you have until you receive more is a general biblical principle that applies to interpretation.

A Sense of Pressure with Words or Scripture

Perhaps the most common way interpretation comes after an utterance is given in an unknown tongue is that a person will experience a feeling of "butterflies" in his stomach or a kind of pressure, or feel that God wants to do something, and then some words or a verse of Scripture will come to mind. If this happens to you, you should give out that verse of Scripture or those words, and then you will move forward with the full interpretation. After this, things will follow that you did not plan and could not have imagined yourself, so that some-times you will be very surprised at what you hear yourself saying.

A GENERAL THOUGHT OR IDEA

Another person may be given a general thought, which he clothes with words of his own choosing. The Holy Spirit does not give the exact words but rather a series of inspired thoughts and leaves it to the person to express it.

HEARING WORDS, SEEING WORDS, SEEING A PICTURE

People may also receive interpretation by actually hear-ing words or seeing them written on a scroll. Others may see a vision or a mental picture and then relate what they see. A Lutheran pastor once came to me and said, "We've had an out-pouring of the Holy Spirit in our church. About fifty or sixty people received the baptism in the Holy Spirit at the altar rails of the church. We are having the gifts of the Spirit in opera-tion. We have what we believe to be interpretation. But we get it in a way that I haven't heard about elsewhere. One person will speak in a tongue, and somebody else will get a kind of mental picture or a vision. They'll start to describe what they have seen in the picture, and it seems to be the interpretation of the tongue." He added, "The funny thing is, all the people in my congregation get it that way. Why is that?"

I replied, "There are things I cannot explain, but I know that people have faith for what they see happen. Jesus said, *'According to your faith be it unto you.'* [Matthew 9:29 KJV] If you believe you are going to receive it one way, that is normally the way you will get it." This is why it is so important to dem-onstrate the gifts of the Spirit for people. Most people do not believe things until they see them. The moment they see it happen, they believe it will happen. To a certain extent, the way we think determines what we experience.

Praying for Interpretation of Tongues

We come now to the question of whether or not we can pray for the interpretation of a tongue. Paul wrote,

> *Even so you, since you are zealous for spiritual gifts, let it be for the edification of the church that you seek to excel. Therefore let him who speaks in a tongue pray that he may interpret.* (1 Corinthians 14:12–13)

The motive with which all the gifts should be put into operation is a desire to edify the body of believers. Paul indicated that since a tongue is more edifying in the public assembly when followed by interpretation, then if you speak in an unknown tongue, you should pray that you may interpret. I have learned by experience that if you can teach people this is God's will and cause them to act upon it, they will invariably receive interpretation. We should remember what Jesus said about asking the Father for something that is good:

> *If a son asks for bread from any father among you, will he give him a stone? Or if he asks for a fish, will he give him a serpent instead of a fish? Or if he asks for an egg, will he offer him a scorpion? If you then, being evil, know how to give good gifts to your children, how much more will your heavenly Father give the Holy Spirit to those who ask Him!* (Luke 11:11–13)

If you are a child of God, and you are prompted or stirred to ask for a certain gift of the Holy Spirit, you are to ask for it, and you will receive what you ask for. Based on this assurance, if you have spoken in an unknown tongue, you desire to interpret, and you have prayed for the interpretation, what do you do next? You just interpret. How do you know you have the right thing? Again, God guarantees that if you ask for the right thing, you will not get the wrong thing. This is faith. It is within the revealed will of God for His people both to speak in tongues and to interpret.

ORDER AND VARIETY IN THE ASSEMBLY OF BELIEVERS

To conclude, let us review a final guideline by Paul concerning the use of the gift of interpretation of tongues.

> *If anyone speaks in a tongue, let there be two or at the most three, each in turn, and let one interpret. But if there is no interpreter, let him keep silent in church, and let him speak to himself and to God.*　　　(1 Corinthians 14:27–28)

Tongues with interpretation should not be overdone in any meeting, just as prophecy should not. No single meeting should be taken over and used exclusively for the operation of any particular gift. God does not want a one-course meal on the table for His children. He gives a variety of nourishment to build up all the members of His body in every way.

CHAPTER 11

Prophecy

n this chapter, we will focus on the third vocal gift, which
is the gift of prophecy or the gift of prophesying. First
Corinthians 12:10 says, *"To another* [is given] *prophecy."*
We have defined this gift as the ability to speak, in a language understood by the believer, words that are inspired
and given by the Holy Spirit. Prophecy is not just inspired
preaching. Neither does it proceed from human reasoning,
learning, education, or seminary training. Like all the other
gifts, it is made possible only by the supernatural operation
of the Holy Spirit.

DESIRE AND SEEK TO PROPHESY

Paul said, *"Follow the way of love and eagerly desire spiritual
gifts, especially the gift of prophecy"* (1 Corinthians 14:1 NIV). I
said earlier the gifts are the way in which love is made effective
and is given expression. This is particularly true of the gift of
prophecy because Paul said prophecy edifies the church. (See
1 Corinthians 14:3–5.) If you love the church, you will want to
edify the church. And in order to edify the church, you will
desire a gift that specifically does that.

Paul's comments that we should *"earnestly desire the best gifts"*
(1 Corinthians 12:31), and that we should *"desire…especially*

the gift of prophecy" (1 Corinthians 14:1 NIV) lead us to consider which of the gifts of the Spirit is *the* best gift. Again, I would say the best gift is the one that best fulfills God's purpose at a given time. The gift you consider to be the best will be relative to the situation and need. Yet, if we had to pick out any one gift that is preeminent over the others, it would apparently be prophecy. This is the only gift we are specifically told in Scripture to earnestly desire and seek. (See also 1 Corinthians 14:39.) Any believer, therefore, who is not interested in and who is not seeking prophecy is really ignoring a scriptural exhortation.

THE SCRIPTURAL BASIS FOR PROPHECY

On the day of Pentecost, Peter said to the crowds, *"This is what was spoken by the prophet Joel: 'In the last days, God says, I will pour out my Spirit on all people'"* (Acts 2:16–17 NIV). God is doing exactly what He said He would do in the last days. He is pouring out His Spirit on all people. Can people of all denominational and nondenominational churches receive the baptism? Can Jews come to receive the baptism? Can Muslims come to receive the baptism? God said *"all people."* Every section of the human race, without exception, is going to experience this last-day visitation of the Holy Spirit.

What did Joel say would happen when the Holy Spirit was poured out?

> *Your sons and daughters **will prophesy**, your young men will see visions, your old men will dream dreams. Even on my servants, both men and women, I will pour out my Spirit in those days, **and they will prophesy**.*

> (Acts 2:17–18 NIV, emphasis added)

Prophecy is particularly emphasized in this passage. In the last days, God's people everywhere are going to have restored to them this beautiful spiritual manifestation of prophesying. We have seen the Holy Spirit poured out today, and we are going to see this on a far more extensive and dramatic scale than most of us yet realize. Four groups are mentioned in verse seventeen, one of which is old men, while the other three are all young: sons, daughters, and young men. In the United States and around the world, we will see a sovereign visitation of God upon young people. They are not going to receive a partial gospel; they are not going to accept mere theological platitudes. Young people today want reality, and God says what He has in store for them is to prophesy and to have visions, dreams, and revelations.

In the last days, God's Spirit will be poured out even more.

Note also that women are included in prophesying: *"your sons and daughters will prophesy"* (Acts 2:17 NIV), and *"even on my servants, both men and women, I will pour out my Spirit"* (v. 18 NIV). We know from the first chapter of Acts that among those who waited with the disciples in the upper room were Mary, the mother of Jesus, and other women. (See Acts 1:14.) They were all baptized in the Holy Spirit, and everything that is written in the second chapter of Acts applied to them.

Prophesying is a ministry that is open to women just as much as it is to men. In Acts we read that *"Philip the evangelist...had four unmarried daughters who prophesied"* (Acts 21:8–9 NIV). Considering the culture of the East, it is extremely improbable that Philip would have four unmarried daughters who were much older than fifteen. In most cases, they would marry when they were about fifteen or sixteen. Some of Philip's daughters were probably even younger than teenagers. I think this is a fairly definite indication that even the children prophesied. I have seen this happen. Many times, my wife Lydia and I witnessed children receiving very beautiful ministry and manifestations of the gift of prophecy.

In 1 Corinthians 11:5, Paul clearly indicated the ministry of prophecy as being open to women. *"Every woman who prays or prophesies with her head uncovered dishonors her head."* Obviously, since Paul required a woman to have her head covered when prophesying, he expected women to be prophesying.

THE NATURE OF PROPHECY

In 1 Corinthians 14:3–4, Paul laid down the basic purposes and functions of the gift of prophecy: *"But he who prophesies speaks edification and exhortation and comfort to men. He who speaks in a tongue edifies himself, but he who prophesies edifies the church."*

We can therefore summarize the differences between prophecy and speaking in an unknown tongue in three ways:

Prophecy

1. Speaks to people
2. Speaks words understood by speaker and hearers
3. Edifies the church

Unknown Tongue

1. Speaks to God
2. Speaks mysteries
3. Edifies individual believers

A failure to understand these purposes has led many people to a wrong understanding of prophecy and even to misuse the gift. The following indicate the general tenor and nature of true prophesying in the New Testament church.

Given for People

Paul said, *"He who prophesies speaks...to men"* (1 Corinthians 14:3). He was contrasting what he had previously said about speaking in an unknown tongue, that *"he who speaks in a tongue does not speak to men but to God"* (v. 2). The primary purpose of prophecy is to speak to people words from God.

Directed at Believers

Which people in particular are being spoken to? The church, or the assembled company of believers. Later in 1 Corinthians 14, Paul wrote, *"Therefore tongues are for a sign, not to those who believe but to unbelievers; but prophesying is not for unbelievers but for those who believe"* (v. 22).

In the first part of this verse, Paul was referring to the particular function of tongues as a supernatural sign to unbelievers, where a believer by the Holy Spirit speaks a language he does not understand but that is understood by an unbeliever who is present. In this way, God brings supernatural conviction to the unbeliever. Again, this is not the regular use of tongues; it is an occasional or exceptional use. In the second part of the verse, Paul was saying that prophesying is not used by God to speak to unbelievers but to minister to believers. This is a very important and basic fact. God does not speak to believers in the way He might speak to unbelievers.

In this respect, prophesying in the New Testament differs from prophesying in the Old Testament, where God often used His prophets to speak to people who were complete unbelievers. For instance, Elijah was used to deliver messages to men who made no real profession of faith. Jeremiah was given messages that went to all the Gentile nations surrounding Israel. We must therefore observe a distinction between Old Testament prophesying and New Testament prophesying in the church, which is the body of Christ. New Testament prophesying is addressed to God's redeemed people, and the tone of it will always be appropriate to God's people.

We should note Paul did say in 1 Corinthians 14:24–25, *"If all prophesy, and an unbeliever or an uninformed person comes in, he is convinced by all, he is convicted by all. And thus the secrets of his heart are revealed; and so, falling down on his face, he will worship God and report that God is truly among you."* The picture here is of a group of believers ministering to each other in prophecy, and an unbeliever happens to come in. Some of the prophetic utterances or revelation touch him and cause him to realize God knows more about him than he understood, which brings

Prophecy is normally given to minister to believers.

him to conviction and an acknowledgment that God is there. This, however, is the exception. Normally, prophecy is given to minister to believers.

For Edification, Exhortation, and Comfort

What does a person who prophesies speak to the church? *"He...speaks edification and exhortation and comfort to men....He who prophesies edifies the church"* (1 Corinthians 14:3–4). Prophecy is limited to edification, exhortation, and comfort because God does not discourage and beat down believers. As I mentioned above, He does not pour forth warnings of judgment against believers, but unbelievers.

Let us look a little more closely at these three primary purposes of prophesying.

The first purpose is to edify. This word may seem a little old-fashioned and ecclesiastical-sounding to many people. However, most people are still familiar with the term *edifice*, which is a building. To edify simply means "to build up or strengthen." It means to make people more effective as members of the body of Christ in whatever particular ministries they have. If you receive the gift of prophesying, then, it should make you better able to serve the Lord and His people.

The second purpose is to exhort, which means "to stimulate, to encourage, to admonish, and to stir up." Admonishment can include severe warning and even rebuke. However, exhortation does not include condemnation. *"There is therefore now no condemnation to those who are in Christ Jesus, who do not walk according to the flesh, but according to the Spirit"* (Romans 8:1).

The third purpose is to comfort, which, in contemporary words, means "to cheer up."

True Prophecy Never Brings Condemnation

I mentioned above that true prophecy, and exhortation in particular, do not bring condemnation. I want to emphasize this point again because, over the years, I have heard many instances of people claiming to prophesy, yet the total effect could be summed up as confusion and condemnation. That is not a genuine manifestation of the Holy Spirit. God is never the author of confusion, nor does the Holy Spirit ever minister condemnation to the people of God. Much of what is called prophecy and prophesying among some believers is not the real thing. It does not serve the primary purposes of edification, exhortation, and comfort.

Unfortunately, some people feel the more they can beat people down and leave them feeling useless, worthless, and condemned—including themselves—the more spiritual they are. The absolute opposite is the truth. Years ago, I used to think if I could leave everybody feeling how terrible they were, I had done a tremendous job of preaching. Then the Holy Spirit took hold of me and showed me I was a failure as a preacher. The Holy Spirit does not leave people feeling terrible, and this is not to be the object of preaching or ministering.

Prophecy is for edification, exhortation, and comfort.

True prophesying does not serve the devil's purpose; it *undoes* the devil's purpose. If so-called prophesying condemns and discourages, it is doing the devil's work. Two of Satan's greatest and most frequently used weapons against God's people are condemnation and discouragement. I heard Billy Graham quote somebody who said that God never uses a discouraged man. I can well believe that, because a discouraged man is not someone who is under the influence of the Holy Spirit, who does not discourage believers. It is extremely important for us to understand this. If an influence, suggestion, or message comes into your life that has the effect of discouraging you, do not attribute it to the Holy Spirit.

One of the problems is that many Christians believe they are being humble when they feel condemned and subsequently go around telling people how bad they are. Yet, when you are a new creation in Jesus Christ and are God's handiwork, every time you criticize yourself, you are criticizing God's work. You are not glorifying God; you are glorifying the devil.

It is the devil who makes people feel guilty. We read in 2 Corinthians 5:19 that *"God was in Christ reconciling the world to Himself, not imputing their trespasses to them, and has committed to us the word of reconciliation."* God has committed to us the word of reconciliation, not condemnation. It is not spiritual to go around making everybody feel how sinful they are; it doesn't do them any good. We should go around making people understand God wants to help them, He loves them, and He is on their side. God is not against anybody. He is not against the Chinese, the Russians, the Arabs, the Europeans, or the Americans. He is for the human race, and this is the message of the gospel. It is the good news.

The principle of no condemnation in Christ (see Romans 8:1) is very important for us to understand, and it applies particularly to prophecy. If believers could live in this place of no condemnation, the church would be an army the devil could not overcome. As I said, the greatest single weapon the devil has against believers is a sense of condemnation, unworthiness, failure, and discouragement. Yet one of the great instruments God has placed at the disposal of believers to overcome these things is the gift of prophecy, which builds up and encourages. This is why it is a tragedy to see prophecy misused to do the very thing it is supposed to counteract!

Prophecy Comes through Our Comforter

Jesus called the Holy Spirit the Comforter. (See, for example, John 14:16, 26 KJV.) We should bear in mind that the Holy Spirit's relationship to the redeemed of God is as our Comforter. The Greek word *parakletos*, translated *"Comforter,"* *"Helper"* (NKJV), or *"Counselor"* (NIV) is closely related to the word translated *"exhortation"* in 1 Corinthians 14. *Parakletos* means "one called in alongside you." The Holy Spirit's business is to encourage, stir up, stimulate, cheer up, help, and counsel. It is most literally translated in English as *advocate,* which is from a Latin word meaning "one called in." You do not call in an advocate or an attorney to condemn you—you would be very foolish to pay him for that—but to plead your cause for you. What would be the use of hiring an attorney who set out to prove in court how guilty you were? You would not feel he was doing his job.

Likewise, the Holy Spirit is called in and sent by God to help you. He comes to justify you on the basis of your redemption in Christ, not condemn you. The Holy Spirit is the best attorney. He comes from the very best place, He is sent by our best friend Jesus, and He comes to plead our cause. Therefore, do not accept condemnation or discouragement. Again, anything that causes you to feel fearful and unworthy is not the voice of the Holy Spirit.

Prophecy Gives a Word in Season

Prophecy can give a word in season to those who are spiritually, emotionally, and physically weary. Let us look at two very beautiful Scriptures that relate to this attribute of prophecy. Proverbs 15:23 says, *"A man has joy by the answer of his mouth, and a word spoken in due season, how good it is!"* In Isaiah, we have one of the most beautiful pictures of Jesus in the Old Testament. This is what Jesus said prophetically through the prophet: *"The Lord GOD has given Me the tongue of the learned, that I should know how to speak a word in season to him who is weary"* (Isaiah 50:4).

A good mark of true learning is being able to speak a word in season to someone who is weary. I know many people who are educated but not learned, and they certainly are not able to do this. In fact, I find many educated people can be somewhat discouraging. They can tend to look down on you, criticize you, and make you feel inferior. They are so knowledgeable about everything, they know just how bad things are and how they are going to get worse. The Holy Spirit isn't like that. Through Jesus, He gives this precious ability to speak a word in season to those who are weary.

The Holy Spirit gives the ability to speak a word in season to those who are weary.

Prophecy Comes to Those Who Hear

The second half of Isaiah 50:4 reads, *"He awakens Me morning by morning, He awakens My ear to hear as the learned."* You cannot speak if you have not heard. If God does not awaken your ear to hear, you are not going to have anything to minister or speak to others. One of the great secrets of Jesus' ministry that is revealed in this verse is that, morning by morning, He had communion with God the Father. Before Jesus went out and met the multitudes, He was with His Father. He heard the voice of God speaking to Him, giving Him words of comfort and encouragement He could speak to others.

This principle is also stated in Proverbs 21:28: *"A false witness shall perish: but the man that heareth speaketh constantly"* (KJV). To say anything that is worth anything, you have to hear from God before you speak. Your ear has to be awakened before you can speak a word in season. None of the prophets ever ministered before he had first received. Ezekiel was told by God to eat the word He gave him and then to give it forth. (See Ezekiel 3:1.) This applies to the gift of prophecy today. Ministering in the Spirit does not come off the top of your head. You have to take the Word into your spirit so you can minister it out of your spirit. The person who has never received anything into his spirit never has anything to minister out of his spirit.

Prophecy Comes through Self-Denial

Second Corinthians 4:12 says, *"So then death is working in us, but life in you."* If we are going to minister life to others, we also have to let death "work" in us. We have to die to our own self-will, our own ideas, and our own determination. We have to open up a channel that the will and the Spirit of God can work through.

One of the wonderful themes of 2 Corinthians is *comfort,* which, as we have seen, is one of the great words connected with the Holy Spirit and with prophecy. At the beginning of the epistle, Paul wrote these beautiful words: *"Blessed be the God and Father of our Lord Jesus Christ, the Father of mercies and God of all comfort..."* (2 Corinthians 1:3). Anything that is comforting, encouraging, and uplifting has its origin in God. He is the God of *all* comfort.

Paul went on to speak about the tremendous tribulations, persecutions, and trials he and his companions were experiencing, using the words *comfort, comforted,* or *consolation* five times:

> ...who comforts us in all our tribulation, that we may be able to comfort those who are in any trouble, with the comfort with which we ourselves are comforted by God. For as the sufferings of Christ abound in us, so our consolation also abounds through Christ.   (2 Corinthians 1:4–5)

He said the pressure against them was so fierce they had no way to measure it. They did not have the strength to resist it; it pressed them to the very point of extinguishing life. *"For we do not want you to be ignorant, brethren, of our trouble which came to us in Asia: that we were burdened beyond measure, above strength, so that we despaired even of life"* (v. 8).

God *did* deliver, He *does* deliver, and He *will* deliver!

Then Paul gave this beautiful statement: *"Yes, we had the sentence of death in ourselves, that we should not trust in ourselves but in God who raises the dead, who delivered us from so great a death, and does deliver us; in whom we trust that He will still deliver us"* (vv. 9–10). Note Paul mentioned deliverance in three tenses: past, present, and future. He did deliver, He does deliver, and He will deliver. That is a message of comfort!

Likewise, until we come to the place where we have the "sentence of death" in ourselves, we do not have this ability to minister comfort to others. The one who will really minister comfort must have experienced the death of his selfish, self-pleasing ego. Yet it is a blessed privilege to have been through this. I understand it to be the inner working of prophecy in the human spirit.

I emphasize this because, again, I have seen prophecy greatly misused and cheapened so it is almost a means to display a human personality rather than minister to the needs of others. The purpose of prophecy is not to make you a dictator. It is not to enable you to go around pointing your finger at people and saying, "Thus saith the Lord...." It is to minister comfort to people. It is also to edify and to build up in order to make believers better equipped and able to serve the Lord and to fulfill their place and function in the body of Christ.

PROPHECY AND OTHER GIFTS OF THE SPIRIT

Let us now look at the relationship between prophecy and other vocal and revelation gifts.

Prophecy and Tongues

First, as I wrote previously, speaking in tongues often leads into prophecy. We saw in Acts 19:6 that, after the disciples at Ephesus had been ministered to by Paul and had been baptized in the name of Jesus, *"when Paul had laid hands on them, the Holy Spirit came upon* [down over] *them, and they spoke with tongues and prophesied."* If we do not become inhibited but allow the Holy Spirit to work, very frequently, speaking with tongues will lead into prophesying. I am sure this happened on the day of Pentecost, and it happened in Ephesus.

Prophecy and Words of Wisdom and Knowledge

Prophecy may also become a vehicle for other related gifts. We know that the gifts are like the colors of the rainbow. Though we can distinguish different colors, we cannot say at any specific point where one color ends and another begins. Likewise, prophecy can blend into other gifts, such as a word of knowledge or a word of wisdom. A word of knowledge may be given through an utterance that is prophesied. In this case, more than one gift is operating at the same time.

For example, you can pour a black fluid made from coffee beans into a cup and say it is a cup of coffee, and that would be true. Yet suppose you offer a cup of coffee to someone and ask, "Do you take sugar and cream?" If he says yes, and you put in sugar and cream, you still call it coffee. Yet the black fluid has become a vehicle for the cream and sugar. In the same way, what we call prophecy is sometimes prophecy alone, and sometimes it is prophecy containing a word of wisdom or a word of knowledge. We still call it prophecy, but we have to acknowledge another element in it.

More than one gift can be in operation at the same time.

Acts 13:2 says, *"As they* [five prophets and teachers in the church at Antioch] *ministered to the Lord and fasted, the Holy Spirit said, 'Now separate to Me Barnabas and Saul for the work to which I have called them.'"* We are not told how the Holy Spirit made this statement, but it seems more than probable it was given through prophecy. It would appear the prophecy was not given through Barnabas or Saul because they are referred to in the third person. One of the other three men therefore had this utterance in prophecy. Yet note the utterance was really more than prophecy. It was a directive word of wisdom revealing the will and plan of God and who was to go forth.

In Acts 20, we have Paul's testimony regarding what had been happening during his journey to Jerusalem. He told the elders of Ephesian church, whom he had called to the port of Miletus, *"And see, now I go bound in the spirit to Jerusalem, not knowing the things that will happen to me there, except that the Holy Spirit testifies in every city, saying that chains and tribulations await me"* (vv. 22–23). In every place along the way where Paul had fellowshipped with believers, the Holy Spirit had been revealing what lay ahead.

Paul was not specific about how the Holy Spirit had testified in each city. He did, however, use the word *"saying."* It seems extremely reasonable and probable that these utterances came either by way of a tongue followed by interpretation or by way of prophecy. In city after city, as Paul journeyed along on his way to Jerusalem, some brother or sister would come forth with an utterance in prophecy telling him—with some description or another—bonds and afflictions lay ahead of him in Jerusalem. These were words of knowledge regarding what Paul was to experience.

More of these revelations came as he continued on his journey after Miletus. Paul and his companions arrived at the port of Tyre, *"and finding disciples,…stayed there seven days. They told Paul through the Spirit not to go up to Jerusalem"* (Acts 21:4). The phrase *"told Paul through the Spirit"* could mean a word of wisdom or it could mean prophecy containing a word of wisdom. Whatever the exact gift was, the result was that Paul was detained and restrained from going up to Jerusalem.

After Tyre, Paul went to Caesarea, where a prophet named Agabus came down from Judea to visit him. *"When he had come to us, he took Paul's belt, bound his own hands and feet, and said, 'Thus says the Holy Spirit, "So shall the Jews at Jerusalem bind the man who owns this belt, and deliver him into the hands of the Gentiles'"'"* (Acts 21:11).

Paul's journey to Jerusalem was rather like going through a series of traffic lights. He came to one place after another and the light was red—stop. He stopped there and waited, the light turned green, and he went on to the next place, where the light was red. He waited, and the light turned green. And so on. We see that all through this section of Paul's life and ministry, the Spirit was bearing witness through other believers, in a combination of prophecy and other gifts, of what lay ahead. God worked through believers whose names are not given, in congregations about which we know very little. Yet these beautiful gifts of the Spirit were actually helping and directing Paul in his ministry.

Prophecy and related gifts also played a very important part in the ministry of Timothy. Paul wrote to Timothy, who was fulfilling a God-given ministry in the city of Ephesus, *"This charge I commit to you, son Timothy, according to the prophecies previously made concerning you, that by them you may wage the good warfare"* (1 Timothy 1:18). Apparently, in various places in the past—possibly in his home assembly, which was in Lystra—prophecies had been given forth in relation to Timothy. These prophecies said he was to fulfill a certain ministry, warned him that he would meet opposition and difficulty, and told him he would have to go ahead. When he entered into this ministry and encountered these difficulties, he could be strengthened by the remembrance of the prophecies that had gone before him.

This kind of encouragement and strengthening is one of the workings of prophecy. Suppose you receive a revelation of the will of God, you step into His will, and then the going gets very hard as the opposition becomes tough. You may think, "Perhaps I'm in the wrong place," or "Maybe I won't make it through this." Then you can think, *No, I have that word of prophecy. It told me I was going to go this way and I would meet opposition. I am just experiencing what is necessary in doing God's will.*

In 1 Timothy 4:14, Paul wrote in a similar vein when he said, *"Do not neglect the gift that is in you, which was given to you by prophecy with the laying on of the hands of the eldership."* The Greek word translated *"gift"* is *charisma*. As I pointed out in chapter one, this word has many different meanings. It may mean a spiritual gift, or it may mean a ministry. It probably refers to an apostolic ministry because it was scriptural for the apostle to be sent forth from the congregation with the laying on of the hands of the elders. At a time when Timothy was facing opposition and difficulty, Paul was reminding him not to forget he was set apart to this ministry by prophecy with the laying on of the hands of the elders. If you

Don't neglect the gift that is in you. God has revealed His will, so fulfill it.

read between the lines of this epistle, you will see Paul was continually stirring Timothy up, saying, in essence, "Don't get discouraged; don't give up. Don't neglect the gift that is in you. Don't give way to fear. God has called you to this ministry. He has revealed His will, so follow through and fulfill it." This is one of the themes of both epistles to Timothy.

I wrote another book in which I referred to the laying on of hands for a gift. I pointed out what we have been discussing in this chapter—that people sometimes receive prophecies that show them the way their lives will take and that, in moments of difficulty, they should be reminded of these prophecies for encouragement and strengthening. After the book was first printed, I met a pastor in New Zealand who said, "I want to tell you that your book came into my hands and did exactly that for me. When I was in the United States at Bible school, prophecies were given out that I would have a particular ministry and fulfill a certain job. I got here to New Zealand and things became sticky. I became rather discouraged and nothing was happening. I got your book and I read this passage about prophecies that have gone before and how Timothy was stirred up to do the task. When I read that in the book, I remembered the prophecies that had gone on before me in the United States. I saw that I wasn't fulfilling my ministry, and it stirred me up to do it."

Since then, God has wonderfully blessed that man as he took a step forward in faith, and he has entered fully into the ministry that was prophesied over him. We can see that prophecy was not just an irrelevant frill in his life but an important part in his finding and fulfilling his ministry.

EXERCISING PROPHECY IN A LOCAL ASSEMBLY

Let us conclude by seeing how prophecy is to be exercised in an orderly way in a local assembly so all may benefit from it.

It Is God's Will for All to Prophesy

In chapter one, we discussed the distinction between the ministry of a prophet and the gift of prophesying. The Bible says all may prophesy, but it does not say all will have the specific ministry of prophet. Paul said, *"For you can **all** prophesy one by one"* (1 Corinthians 14:31, emphasis added). It is clearly the revealed will of God for all believers to prophesy. If we do not prophesy, it is not because it isn't God's will. It is because we have not moved into the will of God.

Those Who Prophesy Must Yield to One Another

"You can all prophesy one by one, that all may learn and all may be encouraged" (1 Corinthians 14:31). We are not all to prophesy at once in a meeting because that would cause confusion. We are to prophesy one by one so that all may learn. Some people do not realize we must learn to operate spiritual gifts. Few people ever begin by prophesying perfectly. Paul said if we have the gift of prophecy, *"let us prophesy in proportion to our faith"* (Romans 12:6). We are to do as much as we have faith for and stop there. If we begin to operate in the gift, we will grow and mature in it. If we never begin, we will never mature. Some people will not do a thing unless they can do it perfectly, and the probable result is they will never do it at all.

Paul wrote, *"Let two or three prophets speak, and let the others judge* [discern]. *But if anything is revealed to another who sits by, let the first keep silent"* (1 Corinthians 14:29–30). There is a time to speak and there is a time to stop speaking. My wife Lydia and I saw a clear example of this when we were working with the young people in the teacher-training college in East Africa. In our Sunday evening services, I would preach the Word to them as thoroughly and as carefully as I could for about an hour, and then we would open up the meeting for worship and anything God wanted to do. We would start to praise the Lord, and there would perhaps be an utterance in a tongue, with interpretation, or a prophecy. Then one of these students would put his hand up and say, "Please, sir, the Lord has just told me something." I would say, "Well, if the Lord has told you, don't keep it to yourself. Come up and tell us all." I would then say to the rest of the group, "The Bible says if anything is revealed to another who sits by, let the first keep silent. You be quiet and let's listen."

We had some fascinating things happen that way. One of these involved a young man who had been a real rebel. He had been so troublesome that even the African teachers wanted me to dismiss him. But the Lord took hold of him, and he was converted. About one week after his conversion, he was sitting in the meeting and said, "Please, sir." I replied, "Yes, what is it?" He continued, "The Lord has just told me that there's a verse in the Bible about traffic on the roads today." I said, "Yes, you'll find it in Nahum. I think it is in the second chapter about the chariots jostling one another in the streets." When he found that, he almost fell off his seat with delight.

If we do not prophesy, it is because we have not moved into the will of God.

Think about how the Lord moved in this situation. The Lord did not tell him where the verse was. He told him there was a verse and he had to ask me where the verse was. We had things like that happen quite frequently with those students. I have never been in another situation where I have seen so realistically what this verse means, *"If anything is revealed to another who sits by, let the first keep silent"* (1 Corinthians 14:30). This is the ministry of the members of the body one to another.

As I said in the previous chapter, it is not right to give over a whole meeting to any one manifestation, whether it is tongues and interpretation or prophesying or anything else. We should never let ourselves become tied down to just one type of manifestation. Sometimes, when people first speak in tongues, all they want to do is speak in tongues. When they start to prophesy, all they want to do is prophesy, and so on. We have to be disciplined and not get stuck in a rut. There are many different ways God can move and speak and bless. Let us be open to what He wants to do.

There is one other very important principle regarding prophecy, which we will explore in more detail in the next chapter. First Corinthians 14:32 says, *"The spirits of the prophets are subject to the prophets."* A true prophet does not lose control of himself. He is always accountable to Scripture and the body of Christ for what he says and does. He cannot put the blame on God and say, "I couldn't help it. God made me do it." This is not scriptural. I have heard that weak excuse given many times to justify foolishness. We are accountable for what we do when we are ministering in the Spirit. God does not overrule our wills. He does not force or coerce us. We are responsible to learn how to yield to the Holy Spirit and the body of believers when prophesying.

CHAPTER 12

HOW TO JUDGE *Prophecy*

I n the last chapter, I pointed out it is unbiblical to allow prophesying in an assembly of believers if it is not submitted to scriptural judgment and the discernment of the body of Christ. On the basis of what I have seen over the years, it would be better not to have prophesying at all than to have prophesying that is not checked by scriptural standards. In this chapter, I want to present the various standards of judgment that are presented to us for this purpose in the New Testament.

"Let two or three prophets speak, and let the others judge [discern]*"* (1 Corinthians 14:29). In this verse, the word *"prophets"* may refer to the ministry of a prophet or to believers who exercise the gift of prophesying. The guidelines that follow apply to both situations. I believe *"the others"* in *"let the others judge"* refers to the other prophets present in the assembly, who are qualified to discern the prophecy.

PROPHETS ARE NOT TO ACT ALONE

A significant fact about those who prophesy under the new covenant is that they do not normally operate on their own as individuals. In the New Testament, the word *prophet* is always used in the plural, except for one place. Even there, the context indicates more than one prophet. Prophets in the New Testament

1. are part of the body of Christ.
2. function as members in the body.
3. are related to other members of the body.

This is somewhat in contrast to the Old Testament, where you find a prophet like Elijah, who was a kind of rugged individualist standing out against the background of apostasy and wickedness. The Lord had to show Elijah he was not the only faithful man left in Israel. Yet Elijah was actually functioning as the principal mouthpiece of God at that time to the nation of Israel. The New Testament concept is of a body with many members all operating together and in relationship to one another. No one member can operate effectively on his own.

Prophets in the church, therefore, minister within groups. When one is ministering, the others are exercising judgment, or discernment. Paul said two or three prophets should speak at any one meeting—not all of them—and let the other prophets discern what they say.

An example of a typical New Testament exercise of the prophetic ministry can be seen in Acts 11:27–28: *"And in these days prophets came from Jerusalem to Antioch. Then one of them, named Agabus, stood up and showed by the Spirit that there was going to be a great famine throughout all the world, which also happened in the days of Claudius Caesar."* We read another incident involving Agabus in the last chapter. He prophesied about what would happen to Paul in Jerusalem. Note here that the prophets came in a group: *"prophets came from Jerusalem"* (Acts 11:27). Agabus was given the actual opportunity to minister, and he brought the message God had given, yet he was not an individual operating on his own.

Many believers have gone astray through exercising a prophetic ministry on their own. I have seen this happen. In a number of cases, you actually find people more or less representing themselves as the sole mouthpiece of God to a certain assembly, congregation, or prayer group. Not only is this incorrect, but also the whole attitude is totally contrary to the spirit and purpose of the New Testament. I know of one denomination in which every congregation normally had a set prophet who appointed a set apostle. These two individuals actually ran the congregation.

Again, there are no dictators in the body of Christ. No gift or ministry is intended to create such a dictatorship. There is a sharing together of ministry and of responsibility for that ministry.

THE NATURE OF JUDGING PROPHECY

Prophecy must therefore be subjected to judgment. I do not mean this in the sense of picking the prophecy to pieces, but of discerning whether it is from God, whether it is true, and whether it is something we really need to heed. Paul brought out this truth again in 1 Thessalonians 5:19–21: *"Do not quench the Spirit. Do not despise prophecies. Test all things; hold fast what is good."*

We are not to quench the Holy Spirit by refusing the gifts and manifestations of the Holy Spirit, as some people have done. This usually happens where there has been a misuse of spiritual gifts. For instance, I know a church in Britain that has a sign on the wall in the main auditorium, which says, "No speaking in tongues except in the basement." Speaking in tongues was so misused and overdone they just could not cope with the problem, so they banished it to the basement. Similarly, I know of a congregation in the United States that allows messages in tongues only on Thursdays. We may smile at this, but this is actually the practice of a very large, prominent congregation. These are not scriptural solutions to the problem, although they illustrate there has been a real problem that needs to be addressed. The answer is not to quench the Spirit but to discover scriptural guidelines for the orderly use of spiritual gifts in the assembly of believers.

Search the Scriptures for guidelines in using the spiritual gifts.

Paul said, *"Do not despise prophecies"* (1 Thessalonians 5:20), so there could be situations where people would despise prophecies in a general sense. I have to say frankly that, if the Bible didn't say not to despise prophecies, there have been times I might have despised prophecies because I have heard so many half-baked, useless utterances put forth under the guise of prophecy. I understand why Paul made that statement. The solution to the problem is not to despise prophecies in general or to quench the Holy Spirit. It is to *"test all things; hold fast what is good"* (v. 21). Do not accept all prophesying without question as being from God and being relevant, true, and authoritative. Test it, and retain what is good. When you eat fish, you eat the flesh and discard the bones. Do the same with prophesying. Eat the meat, but do not give yourself indigestion trying to swallow the bones.

The *Gifts* of the Spirit

The apostle John spoke about testing prophecy in 1 John 4:1: *"Beloved, do not believe every spirit, but test the spirits, whether they are of God; because many false prophets have gone out into the world."* The Greek word translated *"test"* in this verse is the same one translated *"test"* in *"test all things"* from 1 Thessalonians 5:21. Notice that a false prophet is one who has a false spirit. When you test prophecy, you are not testing the prophet as an individual, but you are testing the spirit that is speaking through the prophet. We are warned there are many false prophets who have gone out into the world with false spirits operating through them.

In 1 John 4:6, John drew the distinction between the *"spirit of truth"* and the *"spirit of error."* There is a spirit of error, and it will sometimes seek to impart error disguised as prophecy. In fact, I have heard people try to sustain false doctrine by manipulating prophecy. It was very obvious their whole purpose in prophesying was to get you to swallow a doctrine they were trying to put across.

Practical Principles for Testing Prophecy

Let us now look at nine practical principles for judging prophecy. Today, if you go to a doctor to have a condition diagnosed, he will not do what they used to do in the old days. They would just check your pulse, take your temperature, and ask you to stick out your tongue, and if it looked pink, you were healthy. Instead, he will subject you to all sorts of tests related to different organs of the body. Then, when he has been through every test, he will come up with his total diagnosis of your condition. The same approach applies to judging prophecy. You cannot accept just one or two tests. There is a whole battery of tests, and if you really want to be sure, you should work through them and form your judgment only when you have been through them.

Test #1:
Does It Build Up or Condemn?

The first test relates to the purpose of prophecy we discussed in the previous chapter. First Corinthians 14:3 says, *"But he who prophesies speaks edification and exhortation and comfort to men."* Whenever I hear a message that is condemnatory, negative, and destructive, I do not accept it as genuine prophesying because it does not meet the parameters that have been set in this Scripture.

One Sunday, I was to preach to a congregation in Chicago, and I was on the platform waiting to speak as they were going through the praise portion of the service. At the beginning of one of the songs, a man stood up somewhere near the back and started to speak in a rather harsh voice what he obviously wanted us to believe was prophecy. The message that he brought had very little real meaning.

Evaluate prophecy using the complete set of scriptural tests.

What I was able to make of it was a general sense of condemnation and a warning of judgment hanging over people's heads. I sat there on the platform and boiled with anger but did nothing about it. About two hymns later, the man stood up and did the same. This time, I could not sit quietly any longer, so I stood up while he was still speaking, got to the microphone, and said, "I just want to tell you all that I do not accept this as a genuine manifestation of the gift of prophecy because the

Scripture says he who prophesies speaks to men edification, exhortation, and comfort. All I've heard in what our brother has said so far has been condemnation and confusion, which are the exact opposites."

That created something of a stir, as you can imagine. After a little while, another brother who also had the gift of prophecy stood up and said, "I want to offer my opinion, and I agree with Brother Prince. This was not genuine prophesying." Then a third brother stood up and said the same thing, and we had dealt with the situation in a scriptural way. The others had judged; they had given their unanimous verdict, and the man was squelched. I thought he would never come back, but he came back the next Sunday and behaved in a much more respectful and decent way.

But that day, after things had settled down, I said to the people, "I want to tell you one main reason why I did what I did. In the front rows, we have two complete rows of young people [among them teenagers and college students]. While that man was prophesying, I was looking at their faces, and their faces were registering one thing: this is phony. I just want to tell those young people I agree with them; it was phony. I have seen far too many young people turned off from the whole business of the Holy Spirit and the gifts of the Spirit by their elders and so-called betters trying to pretend something that is wrong is right, for the sake of being dignified and decent in church, that I will not go along with it."

Generally speaking, I believe I did the right thing in that situation. Normally, the religious thing would be either to try to sing the man down with choruses or to say a pat, "Amen. Praise the Lord," at the end as if it was all right when it wasn't. I don't believe God is pleased with that. If we permit the exercise of prophesying, we have an obligation placed upon us by Scripture to have the operation of judging or discerning along with it. It is too dangerous to have prophesying without testing. It is like turning a young person loose in a very fast sports car without checking the steering and the brakes. He may end up in a wreck. Over the years, I have seen scores and scores of wrecks through the misuse of prophecy. I have seen homes broken up, churches divided, and people ruined financially and in other ways through the wrong use of prophecy. Prophecy is an extremely powerful instrument, and if it is misused, it can be misused to the destruction of people.

There is a time when God does rebuke and chasten His people. There is a place for this, but it is never His last word. Let us look at the example of Jeremiah. The Lord commissioned him to be a prophet, saying, *"I ordained you a prophet to the nations....I have put My words in your mouth. See, I have this day set you over the nations and over the*

There is a time for rooting out and pulling down, but God's ultimate goal is planting.

kingdoms, to root out and to pull down, to destroy and to throw down, to build and to plant" (Jeremiah 1:5, 9–10). There is a time for rooting out and pulling down what God has not planted. Jesus said, *"Every plant which My heavenly Father has not planted will be uprooted"* (Matthew 15:13). Yet the ultimate purpose is planting. Likewise, there is a place for knocking down and destroying, but the ultimate purpose is building. If we never reach the positive, we are not moving with the Holy Spirit. His dealings with the people of God are always good and positive, with the purpose of building up.

Paul echoed this principle in 2 Corinthians. He had to use fairly stern language in correcting the Corinthian church, and he also had to assert his own authority, which was in question. After doing so, he said, *"For even if I should boast somewhat more about our authority, which the Lord gave us for edification and not for your destruction, I shall not be ashamed"* (2 Corinthians 10:8). Notice the authority given to Paul as an apostle was for edification, not destruction. In a later chapter, Paul used parallel language: *"Therefore I write these things being absent, lest being present I should use sharpness, according to the authority which the Lord has given me for edification and not for destruction"* (2 Corinthians 13:10).

We must bear in mind the Holy Spirit will use conviction in correcting us, but there is a great difference between condemnation and conviction. Conviction is specific. If you told a lie or stole money, He will convict you that you must make amends or take it back and apologize. Conviction is never vague or obscure; it always leads you with something specific you have to do. Condemnation will be vague. If you nail one of the devil's accusations, he will come up with two more. If you nail these two, he has four more. Whenever you get into the area of condemnation, you are outside the operation of the Holy Spirit and you are letting the devil play with you like a cat plays with a mouse. Unfortunately, it is often preachers or people who claim to minister who are doing this part of the devil's job for him.

Test #2:
Does It Agree with Scripture?

The second test is whether the prophecy agrees with Scripture. This scriptural test is very important. Second Timothy 3:16 says, *"All Scripture is given by inspiration of God, and is profitable for doctrine, for reproof, for correction, for instruction in righteousness.*" The authority behind all Scripture is the Holy Spirit, and He will never contradict Himself. Anything given in prophecy, therefore, will never be opposed to the letter or the spirit of Scripture. Paul wrote about the consistency of God's Word when he declared,

> *Do I make my plans in a worldly manner so that in the same breath I say, "Yes, yes" and "No, no"? But as surely as God is faithful, our message to you is not "Yes" and "No." For the Son of God, Jesus Christ, who was preached among you by me and Silas and Timothy, was not "Yes" and "No," but in him it has always been "Yes." For no matter how many promises God has made, they are "Yes" in Christ.*
>
> (2 Corinthians 1:17–20 NIV)

In other words, God does not say one thing on one day and another thing on another day.

These words from Isaiah are also very applicable as we look at the scriptural test of prophecy: *"And when they say to you, 'Seek those who are mediums and wizards* [fortune-tellers or soothsayers], *who whisper and mutter,' should not a people seek their God? Should they seek the dead on behalf of the living?"* (Isaiah 8:19). If you want an answer, do you need to go anywhere but to God? If you want to find the living, should you go to the dead? This passage speaks particularly about attempted communion with the dead, which is not a new practice, and which has always been under the curse of almighty God from the time it was first manifested. Here is God's answer: *"To the law and to the testimony!* [To the written word of God.] *If they do not speak according to this word, it is because there is no light in them"* (v. 20). If they do not speak according to the Scripture, the spirit that is in them and speaks through them is not the Holy Spirit. The Spirit of all true prophecy is the Holy Spirit.

Test #3:
What Is the Prophet's Relationship with Christ?

The third test is the prophet's relationship with Jesus Christ. John 16:13–14 says, *"However, when He, the Spirit of truth, has come, He will guide you into all truth; for He will not speak on His own authority, but whatever He hears He will speak; and He will tell you things to come."* Another specific characteristic of the Holy Spirit is that He always glorifies the Lord Jesus Christ. It is true He will reveal to us things to come, but He will always do this in the context of glorifying Jesus. Whenever anybody comes to you with any kind of revelation or new doctrine or prophecy, ask yourself, *What is this person's attitude to the Lord Jesus Christ? Does he exalt and glorify Him? Does he give Him the preeminence that is due to Him alone?*

The apostle John wrote in Revelation, *"And I fell at his feet to worship him* [the angel]. *But he said to me, 'See that you do not do that! I am your fellow servant, and of your brethren who have the testimony of Jesus. Worship God! For the testimony of Jesus is the spirit of prophecy'"*(Revelation 19:10). The spirit in all true prophecy—from the very first prophecy given to the last prophecy that will ever be given—centers on testifying to Jesus Christ. Anything that departs from testifying to and exalting Jesus Christ is not given by the Holy Spirit.

People have various substitutes for Jesus instead of giving Him the supremacy in their lives. Some will put a human personality, teacher, or preacher above Him. Others will give first place to a denomination, a particular church, or a group. If you ever meet a group that says, "If you want to be right, you must join us," you can be sure of one thing: when you have joined them, you are wrong! Any group having that kind of spirit is wrong to begin with.

In Colossians 1:18, we read, *"And [Jesus] is the head of the body, the church, who is the beginning, the firstborn from the dead, that in all things He may have the preeminence." "All things"* includes prophecy.

Test #4:
Do the Prophet and Prophecy Bear Good Fruit?

The fourth test of prophecy is its fruit. Galatians 5:22–23 has a beautiful, nine-fold list of the fruit of the Spirit: *"love, joy, peace, longsuffering, kindness, goodness, faithfulness, gentleness, self-control."* We therefore need to ask this question: Do the prophet and the prophecy correspond to these qualities of the Spirit?

In Romans 14:17, we have a very clear statement of what the kingdom of God and the gospel are all about. *"For the kingdom of God is not eating and drinking, but righteousness and peace and joy in the Holy Spirit."* The kingdom of God is not a set of institutional rules about what you must eat and not eat, what you must wear and not wear, the places you may go and the places you may not go. It consists of three things: righteousness, peace, and joy in the Holy Spirit.

Notice that righteousness comes first. Any form of presentation of joy and peace that bypasses righteousness is a deception. I have been with many groups that wanted to get happy, clap their hands, praise the Lord, and have a good time, but I have learned that in the end, this can be just self-deception. Much of the happiness we see in some groups is really nothing but soulishness because it is not based on the requirements of God concerning righteousness. Sometimes, we talk so much about the Holy Spirit we forget He is holy. He is the Spirit of holiness.

I have encountered spurious people trying to make others happy without getting them to live according to God's Word. This does not produce the results God has promised. His order is righteousness, peace, and joy in the Holy Spirit.

Jesus specifically warned us about bad fruit in Matthew 7:15: *"Beware of false prophets, who come to you in sheep's clothing, but inwardly they are ravenous wolves."* The sheep

God's order is righteousness, peace, and joy in the Holy Spirit.

represents the Christian disciple. A wolf is a natural enemy of sheep and comes to destroy them. What is the purpose of the wolf putting on sheep's clothing? To pass itself off as a sheep in order to prey on them. The wolf would not be as dangerous if it came as itself, undisguised. It is dangerous when it comes wearing sheep's cloth-ing. This is the nature of many false prophets. They will not tell you what they really believe. They will come to you professing to be Christians, professing to have the message of the gospel, probably professing to have a higher revelation and to bring you into a new experience you have never had before.

It takes a sheepdog to discern the wolf lurking among the sheep. The sheepdog does not judge by its sight but by its sense of smell. In the Bible, the sense of smell can represent a type of the discernment of the Holy Spirit. Those who are responsible for caring for God's flock need to cultivate this extra sense that detects the wolf even when he is wearing the nice, white sheepskin. Yet Jesus revealed, apart from this sense of discernment, an objective way to test whether a prophet is true or false. After He warned against false prophets, He said, *"You will know them by their fruits. Do men gather grapes from thornbushes or figs from thistles?"* (Matthew 7:16). If every time you reach out for fruit, you are jabbed by a sharp thorn, then don't expect a grape. And do not call the plant a grapevine because a vine does not produce thistles.

Although the following is certainly not an exhaustive list, here are some of the most common forms of fruit that are not the fruit of the Holy Spirit, which we should learn to discern. I have observed one or more of these in the lives of people who claim to be preachers, evangelists, ministers, or prophets of Jesus Christ: pride, arrogance, boastfulness, exaggeration or dishonesty, covetousness, financial irresponsibility, addictive appetite, immorality, broken marriage vows, and broken homes. When a guest preacher comes to town next time, ask yourself, Is he going to skip town with somebody's car or somebody's wife? Does he pay his debts or does he walk out and leave somebody else to pay them? There are many important questions to be asked of visiting ministers. If you do not ask them, you may be sorry someday.

Jesus followed up His warnings about false prophets and false fruit with these sobering words:

> *Not everyone who says to Me, "Lord, Lord," shall enter the kingdom of heaven, but he who does the will of My Father in heaven. Many will say to Me in that day, "Lord, Lord, have we not prophesied in Your name, cast out demons in Your name, and done many wonders in Your name?" And then I will declare to them, "I never knew you; depart from Me, you who practice lawlessness!"* (Matthew 7:21–23)

Remember the difference between gifts and fruit—between being given a gift and developing the character of Christ over time. It is possible to cast out demons in the name of Jesus and be living wrong. It is possible to prophesy and be living wrong. It is possible to do miracles and be living with somebody else's wife, embezzling money, or telling lies. I know

There is only one evidence that a person is living right: he is living right.

of people who have done it and are doing it. The authority is in the name of Jesus and in faith, and God has committed Himself to act when any person does something in faith and the name of Jesus. Therefore, the fact that a person prophesies, preaches, casts out demons, and performs miracles does not prove he is living right. There is only one sure evidence a person is living right: he is actually living right. People who do not live

right will not get to heaven. It is that simple. We have allowed a lot of sentimentality and lax thinking to obscure the issue.

The apostle Peter warned about false teachers in his second epistle:

> *But these, like natural brute beasts made to be caught and destroyed, speak evil of the things they do not understand, and will utterly perish in their own corruption, and will receive the wages of unrighteousness, as those who count it pleasure to carouse in the daytime. They are spots and blemishes, carousing in their own deceptions while they feast with you, having eyes full of adultery and that cannot cease from sin, enticing unstable souls. They have a heart trained in covetous practices, and are accursed children. They have*

forsaken the right way and gone astray, following the way of Balaam the son of Beor, who loved the wages of unrighteousness. (2 Peter 2:12–15)

These false teachers attend the Christian love feasts, and may even take part in the Lord's Supper, but they are unclean and vile. It is remarkable how people in a congregation will swallow any kind of lie. You would not think people could believe the things they believe. They will believe anything but the truth.

Peter said these supposed teachers have hearts *"trained in covetous practices"* and follow *"the way of Balaam."* In other words, they are after money. This was Balaam's problem. Wasn't Balaam a prophet? Yes. If you read Numbers 23–25, I do not think you will find more beautiful prophecies in the Bible than came from the lips of Balaam. Yet his heart was not right.

Balaam appears in only three chapters in the Old Testament, but he is referred to several times in the New Testament as an example of warning. Balak, the king of the Moabites, had told Balaam to curse Israel. However, he could not do it because when he prophesied, he could not speak anything but the truth. He could only speak what the Lord gave him to say. Balaam expressed an apparently godly wish that never came true. He said, *"Who can count the dust of Jacob, or number one-fourth of Israel? Let me die the death of the righteous, and let my end be like his!"* (Numbers 23:10).

This was just a pious aspiration. Balaam was greedy, and money was more important to him than living a righteous life. He was killed by the children of Israel. In the book of Joshua, we read about the children of Manasseh when they moved into their inheritance east of Jordan. *"The children of Israel also killed with the sword Balaam the son of Beor, the soothsayer, among those who were killed by them"* (Joshua 13:22). Balaam did not die the death of the righteous, but he also did not live the life of the righteous. Desire for money led him astray. As I wrote earlier, using a gift for personal profit is a temptation for those who operate in certain realms of spiritual gifts and power. We must always take a prophet's fruit and character into consideration when evaluating a prophecy and its effects.

Test #5:
Were the Prophet's Predictions True?

If prophecy contains predictions concerning the future, and these are not fulfilled, the prophecy did not come from God. Let us look at a passage from the book of Deuteronomy. The Lord said,

> *The prophet who presumes to speak a word in My name, which I have not commanded him to speak, or who speaks in the name of other gods, that prophet shall die. And if you say in your heart, "How shall we know the word which the LORD has not spoken?"; when a prophet speaks in the name of the LORD, if the thing does not happen or come to pass, that is the thing which the LORD has not spoken; the prophet has spoken it presumptuously; you shall not be afraid of him.*
>
> (Deuteronomy 18:20–22)

A person may make a prediction that does not come to pass. The Word of God says very simply and practically this was not something the Lord spoke because, if the Lord had spoken it, it would have come to pass. We are not to be afraid of such a prophet. Under the law of Moses, the prophet would have died; that is how God regards those who deceive His people.

We should realize that a person who prophesies can fall into error by overstepping the bounds of his gift. He begins in the right way but goes too far. Paul wrote, *"Having then gifts differing according to the grace that is given to us, let us use them: if prophecy, let us prophesy in proportion to* [by the measure of] *our faith"* (Romans 12:6). People may start prophesying in the Spirit and get excited, puffed up, enthusiastic, and go beyond what the Holy Spirit actually gave them. I have known of cases of this. The people were not out to deceive; they were not false prophets, but they moved out of the Spirit and back into the flesh.

God warns us about this. Just before Paul talked about prophesying in proportion to our faith, he wrote, *"For I say, through the grace given to me, to everyone who is among you, not to think of himself more highly than he ought to think* [don't get puffed up], *but to think soberly, as God has dealt to each one a measure of faith"* (v. 3). You can operate perfectly within the measure of faith God has given you. Yet if you go beyond that measure of faith, you are not operating in the Spirit; you are operating in your own carnal will and personality.

Test #6:
Does the Prophecy Promote Obedience to God?

This test is essential because the fifth test said if the prophecy does not come to pass, we are dealing with a false prophet. We might easily conclude, therefore, that if what the prophet said *does* come to pass, he must be a true prophet. Yet this is not necessarily the case. Even if prophecy contains correct predictions or supernatural revelations, it is not from God if its effect is to promote disobedience against God and the Scriptures.

We are warned about this in Deuteronomy:

If there arises among you a prophet or a dreamer of dreams, and he gives you a sign or a wonder, and the sign or the wonder comes to pass, of which he spoke to you, saying, "Let us go after other gods"; which you have not known; "and let us serve them," you shall not listen to the words of that prophet or that dreamer of dreams, for the LORD your God is testing you to know whether you love the LORD your God with all your heart and with all your soul. You shall walk after the LORD your God and fear Him, and keep His commandments and obey His voice, and you shall serve Him and hold fast to Him. But that prophet or that dreamer of dreams shall be put to death, because he has spoken in order to turn you away from the LORD your God, who brought you out of the land of Egypt and redeemed you from the house of bondage, to entice ["thrust" KJV] you from the way in which the LORD your God commanded you to walk. So you shall put away the evil from your midst. (Deuteronomy 13:1–5)

In this passage, a man gave a supernatural sign and it came to pass. Yet he was a false prophet, a servant of Satan, turning God's people away from their obedience to Him.

I saw something like this in Africa. In a certain village, two families quarreled, which is quite common. One family went to the witch doctor and asked him to put a hex on the other family. After they paid him with a goat, he put the hex on. He said on a certain night in the village a jackal would cry at midnight. When the jackal cried, the youngest child of that family would die. Do you know what happened? The jackal cried, and the baby died. It was exactly as he had said. He had made a correct supernatural prediction. But he was not a servant of God. Even though it came true, he was still a servant of Satan.

Another scriptural example of this is from the ministry of Paul, when he and Silas arrived in Philippi for the first time to preach the gospel. We looked at this incident earlier, in the chapter on discernings of spirits.

> *Now it happened, as we went to prayer, that a certain slave girl possessed with a spirit of divination met us, who brought her masters much profit by fortune-telling. This girl followed Paul and us, and cried out, saying, "These men are the servants of the Most High God, who proclaim to us the way of salvation." And this she did for many days. But Paul, greatly annoyed, turned and said to the spirit, "I command you in the name of Jesus Christ to come out of her." And he came out that very hour.* (Acts 16:16–18)

Everything the girl said was absolutely true. She was apparently the first person in Philippi to fully state who Paul and Silas were. Yet she was a servant of Satan. An evil spirit was causing her to say those things. Notice Satan's cunning in using this girl. Perhaps he wanted to get her in on the ground floor of the new assembly of believers that would come together through the ministry of Paul and Silas. He may have wanted the people of

Even if a prophecy contains correct predictions, it may not be from God.

Philippi to feel there was nothing new in this gospel, that it was just what they were used to with their prophetesses and oracles, which had been part of Greek culture for nine centuries. How

subtle the devil is! He does not always tell out-and-out lies. He would never deceive people if he did. He tells enough truth to get you hooked, and then he injects his lies.

I want to point out one other thing in the above passage from Deuteronomy 13. The King James Version uses the term to *"thrust"* (v. 5) them from the way of the Lord. When a prophecy is false, we may feel a certain kind of pressure that is not from the Holy Spirit. If you come to a place where you feel, "I *must* do that because it was prophesied," do not do it. That is not the way prophecy works.

I had a call from someone who said, "Have you heard any prophecy about resurrection?" When I asked why, he said, "Well, some believers here have a little child that died and everybody is getting prophecies he's going to be raised from the dead." "How long ago did he die?" I asked. "Oh, about three days ago." "What did he die of?" "We don't know." "How old was the boy?" "Six weeks." They had refused to notify the coroner for three days, and he asked me, "What do you think?" I said, "If you want to know what I think, I think that baby is not going to be raised from the dead. The thing I feel about you immediately is a kind of pressure that is not the pressure of the Holy Spirit. You're all under pressure. Take it slowly; be very careful." I heard nothing more. I guarantee the first thing they would have done if the baby had been called back to life would have been to phone me. This has happened among Spirit-baptized people who were seeking to do God's will and be "spiritual." Of course, one sympathizes with people who have lost a little baby, but this is the type of pressure I am referring to.

I have felt this pressure in my own life. If you ever get under that kind of pressure, put on the brakes, get out of the car, and find out what has been driving you because it is not the Holy Spirit.

Test #7:
Does the Prophecy Bring Freedom and Peace?

Paul wrote in 2 Corinthians 3:17, *"Now the Lord is the Spirit; and where the Spirit of the Lord is, there is liberty."* The following Scriptures teach three things that are not products of the Holy Spirit:

> *For you did not receive the spirit of bondage again to fear, but you received the Spirit of adoption by whom we cry out, "Abba, Father."* (Romans 8:15)

> *God is not the author of confusion but of peace.* (1 Corinthians 14:33)

> *God has not given us a spirit of fear, but of power and of love and of a sound mind.* (2 Timothy 1:7)

Bondage, confusion, and fear are not from the Holy Spirit.

We were in a church in Britain where there was a young woman who was about twenty. Somebody had prophesied that this young woman was to marry a young man in the congregation. She didn't love him, and she had no desire to marry him whatsoever. But she was in agony because she thought if she did not marry him, she would be disobeying God and something awful would come in her life. My wife and I explained to her God does not terrify you. He does not send you the spirit of fear, and He will not make you confused. This is not the way the Holy Spirit operates. We helped her be released from this bondage, and her life was probably saved from ruin.

Many times, in churches, particularly in prayer groups, there will be someone—quite often a woman—who will use her prophetic ability to cause people to become dependent on her. She may not be aware of it, but she is making disciples for herself. The people in the group cannot solve their own problems, and they have to go running to Sister So-and-So. This type of arrangement is totally alien to the gospel. In the New Testament, every believer is a priest. Every believer has the right of direct access to God. If you cannot hear directly from God, there is something wrong with your spiritual life, and you need to correct it.

Test #8:
Does the Prophecy Harmonize and Bring Life?

True prophecy given by the Holy Spirit will always inject fresh life into a meeting and harmonize with God's overall purposes. During a meeting, there may be the operation of a gift, such as prophecy, and it will sound very good, very religious, and may even contain Scripture, but it is not of the Holy Spirit. Instead, it is a religious spirit.

The following example concerns the interpretation of tongues, but the same principle applies to prophecy. I was teaching at a businessmen's convention on the gifts of the Spirit, and I was emphasizing the responsibility of the person leading the meeting to take control if anything went wrong. I had just finished speaking and was still the only person on the platform when a woman gave a very beautiful, anointed utterance in a tongue. We waited for the interpretation, and a man stood up and gave what he obviously wanted us to believe was the interpretation. It was all Scripture, such as "'It shall come to pass in the last days,' saith God, 'I will pour out My Spirit,'" and so forth. I can give you the scriptural references for everything he was saying. However, it was stale and dead; it had no life in it, and it was out of line with the whole moving of God in the meeting.

When he finished, I thought, *What do I do now? I have just been telling everybody it is my responsibility to do something.* I believe the Lord really gave me wisdom. I stood up and said very quietly, "A brother has quoted some of the Scriptures that he has memorized. Let's ask God for the interpretation." There was dead silence, and then the interpretation came. It was quick, powerful, and in line with the meeting. It lifted everybody, and there was a spontaneous outburst of praise.

The Holy Spirit is the author of life, not death.

The Holy Spirit is the author of life, not death. He does not deaden. If something is deadening, even though it may sound good and religious, it is not the Spirit of God who is doing it.

Test #9:
Is There a Sense of Warning?

God has put something inside us to enable us to know what is true and what is false. First John 2:27 says, *"But the anointing which you have received from Him abides in you, and you do not need that anyone teach you; but as the same anointing teaches you concerning all things, and is true, and is not a lie, and just as it has taught you, you will abide in Him."* The anointing is not exactly the same as the baptism in the Holy Spirit. It is *walking* in the

Spirit after you have been baptized in the Spirit. When you are walking in the Spirit, there is something inside you that bears witness to the truth and rejects what is false.

When you are in a meeting and gifts come into operation, pay attention to the anointing inside you. Some people get an actual pain in their chest when there is something false. If you get such a warning from God, do not jump up and say, "That man is a false prophet." You will be headed for trouble because it will probably end in an argument. One person will say he believes the one prophesying is right and another will say he is not. This final test is subjective, while the other eight are objective, and you cannot deal with matters in the congregation on the basis of subjective tests. This test is for the purpose of warning you personally. What do you do? If you are warned subjectively by the Spirit within you that something is wrong, just sit there quietly and begin applying the other eight tests. If the person is wrong, one or more of the other tests will show it.

These nine tests for judging true prophecy, therefore, enable believers to operate in this gift with freedom, protection, and the fullness of the Holy Spirit.

PART 5

USING THE *Gifts*

CHAPTER 13

How to Exercise Spiritual

❧❧❧

e conclude our study of the nine supernatural gifts of the Holy Spirit by answering the practical question, How can a believer begin to exercise these gifts in a scriptural way?

The Basis of Exercising Any Gift Is Faith

First, we must understand the basis of all service for God, including the exercise of the gifts of the Holy Spirit. This can be summed up in one simple word: *faith*. Hebrews 11:6 says, *"But without faith it is impossible to please* [God], *for he who comes to God must believe that He is, and that He is a rewarder of those who diligently seek Him."* This is a very clear statement that is often overlooked by religious people. It does not say without *morality* it is impossible to please God; it says without *faith* it is impossible to please God. Of course, God requires moral behavior, but morality by itself does not commend us to Him. Faith is the only basis on which we can be accepted by God.

The Scripture says he who comes to God must believe—must exercise faith. First, he must believe that God exists. Many people believe this, but it is not sufficient in itself. Second, he must believe that God is a rewarder of those who diligently seek Him. In other words, to apply this verse personally, I must believe if I come to God and seek Him diligently according to His Word, He will reward me according to His Word. If I do not believe this, I do not have the right basis on which to approach Him.

The same idea is stated in Romans 14:23, which says, *"Whatever is not from faith is sin."* Anything that is not done in faith is not acceptable to God. It may be a religious activity, such as going to church and singing hymns, or it may even be prayer, but if it is not done in faith it is sin because God has set that one basic requirement from which He will not vary.

If we seek God according to His Word, He will reward us according to His Word.

Since faith is so essential, it is reasonable to ask how we can receive the faith God requires. The answer is found in Romans 10:17: *"So then faith comes by hearing, and hearing by the word of God."* There is a very encouraging thought in this verse: faith *comes*. If you do not have faith, you can obtain it. You do not have to despair and say, "It's no use. I don't have any faith."

I learned this lesson in a very personal way lying in a hospital bed for twelve months during World War II. I said to myself again and again, "I know if I had faith, God would heal me. But it doesn't seem that I have faith." One day, I read a book that contained this Scripture from Romans 10:17. My spirit grasped the statement that faith comes, and it was like a ray of piercing light in the darkness. I realized if I did not have faith, I could get it if I met the condition. The condition was hearing the Word of God.

Hearing is the intermediate stage between the Word of God and faith. It is possible to read the Bible without truly "hearing" it, just as it is possible to hear a sermon and yet not really hear it. Faith does not come until we truly hear what God says in His Word. One great obstacle to hearing is that we already think we know what God is going to say, and so we don't listen if He says something different. This was my problem with healing. When I read what the Bible said about healing, my response was, "That's too good to be true; it couldn't be that way." God had to show me I could not receive faith until I laid down my own opinions, other people's opinions, religious traditions, and denominational teachings and listened to what He was saying to me in His Word. I quieted my spirit, cleared my mind of preconceptions and traditions and prejudices, and just waited for God to speak to my spirit. Then faith began to come, and I was healed.

One of the most important things in the Christian life, therefore, is to cultivate the ability to hear what God is saying in His Word. Cultivating the ability to hear is a process. A person who does not take time in God's presence and in the presence of His Word will not learn to hear.

In regard to spiritual gifts, we need to hear the portions of God's Word that relate to the exercise of these gifts. In this chapter, we will look at eight successive truths from the Word of God that—if you hear them—will build your faith for receiving and exercising the gifts of the Spirit. The following truths are gleaned from what we have learned in the last twelve chapters. You may still have to clear your mind of human traditions, denominational teachings, and personal prejudices, as I did, and be prepared to let God speak to you so you may apply these truths to your life.

Truths That Build Faith for Spiritual Gifts

Truth #1:
The Supreme Purpose of the Gifts
Is to Glorify God

Let us first consider the purpose of spiritual gifts in relation to God. The apostle Peter wrote,

> *As each one has received a gift, minister it to one another, as good stewards of the manifold* [many-sided] *grace of God. If anyone speaks, let him speak as the oracles of God. If anyone ministers, let him do it as with the ability which God supplies, that in all things God may be glorified through Jesus Christ, to whom belong the glory and the dominion forever and ever. Amen.* (1 Peter 4:10–11)

Paraphrasing the above, as each one has received a gift, he should minister it to the others as a good steward of God's grace, which is manifested in these grace gifts of the Spirit. Minister to what purpose? The supreme purpose of the gifts is that God may be glorified through Jesus Christ. Every time we exercise spiritual gifts in accordance with the Word of God, we are bringing glory to God through Jesus Christ. Every time we fail to exercise a spiritual gift when we might have done so, we are robbing God of His glory.

Truth #2:
Ministering Gifts to Believers Brings Edification

Next, let us consider the purpose of spiritual gifts in relation to humanity. We have seen that the purpose of the spiritual gifts is edification, or the building up of believers. The key word of 1 Corinthians 14 is *edify*. As either a verb or a noun, it occurs seven times in the chapter. Let us look at four of these occurrences, three of which we looked at earlier.

> *He who speaks in a tongue edifies himself, but he who prophesies edifies the church* [the assembled company of believers]. (1 Corinthians 14:4)

> *I wish you all spoke with tongues, but even more that you prophesied; for he who prophesies is greater than he who speaks with tongues, unless indeed he interprets, that the church may receive edification.* (v. 5)

> *Even so you, since you are zealous for spiritual gifts, let it be for the edification of the church that you seek to excel.* (v. 12)

> *How is it then, brethren? Whenever you come together, each of you has a psalm, has a teaching, has a tongue, has a revelation, has an interpretation. Let all things be done for edification.* (v. 26)

One of the main means by which Christians are enabled to edify themselves and other believers is by the exercise of spiritual gifts. If we do not exercise the gifts of the Spirit, we are robbing ourselves and others of the means of edification. For example, suppose I am in a group of believers and an utterance is given in an unknown tongue that requires inter-pretation. If I receive the interpretation but, because of fear or embarrassment, I refuse to give it, not only am I robbing myself, but I am also depriving the whole group of believers of the blessing that would have come to them through that interpretation. We should not be guilty of failing to exercise spiritual gifts we could and should be exercising.

Truth #3:
God's Will Is for Believers to Exercise Spiritual Gifts

The third truth is implied in the two previous truths but must still be recognized and acknowledged by individual believers: it is the will of God for believers to exercise spiritual gifts. Operating in the gifts of the Spirit is not something that is confined to a few gifted individuals who are preachers, missionaries, or evangelists. The New Testament clearly depicts every local assembly as made up of believers who are able to exercise spiritual gifts.

Operating in the gifts of the Spirit is not just for preachers, missionaries, or evangelists.

Let us recall what Paul said about the gifts in 1 Corinthians 12: *"The manifestation of the Spirit is given to each one* [believer] *for the profit of all.…But one and the same Spirit works all these things, distributing to each one individually as He wills"* (vv. 7, 11). The emphasis in these verses is on each individual believer receiving and exercising a spiritual gift or gifts for useful, profitable service.

Truth #4:
Love and the Gifts Work Together

Fourth, as we saw in chapter two, there is no conflict between the fruit of love and the gifts of the Spirit. Millions of professing Christians have somehow come to believe love and the gifts are in opposition to one another, as if one excluded the other and a choice has to be made between them. This is completely contrary to Scripture. In 1 Corinthians 12:31,

The Gifts of the Spirit

Paul said, *"Earnestly desire the best gifts. And yet I show you a more excellent way."* A better translation might be, "And I show you a yet more excellent way." Note the placing of the word *"yet"* in the second sentence. The *"more excellent way"* spoken of in the thirteenth chapter of 1 Corinthians is love.

First Corinthians 13:13 says, *"And now abide faith, hope, love, these three; but the greatest of these is love."* Some people say love is the best gift, but this is incorrect. Nowhere does the New Testament call love a gift. Love is a fruit. Some people will tell you love is the best and only gift to be sought, but they are not on scriptural grounds. Paul said we are to earnestly desire the best gifts, even though there is something higher than gifts, which is love. In a certain sense, the *condition* for being shown the more excellent way is to earnestly desire the best gifts. Far from being in opposition to one another, one leads to the other.

Note that Paul led up to the beautiful thirteenth chapter of 1 Corinthians, which deals with the nature of God's love, with the statement, *"Earnestly desire the best gifts. And yet I show you a more excellent way"* (1 Corinthians 12:31). Then, right after the chapter on love, he made this statement: *"Pursue love, **and** desire spiritual gifts"* (1 Corinthians 14:1, emphasis added). He again affirmed both love and gifts. Yet, as I mentioned, some people seem to read the statement as "Pursue love *or* desire spiritual gifts." Paul said to seek love by all means and desire spiritual gifts, and this is perfectly logical because the gifts of the Holy Spirit are channels through which divine love flows. They go hand in hand. They are intimately related, and you cannot really separate one from the other. If you do not have any gifts, you seal off a main channel through which love operates, for love must have a means of expression.

To talk about love but do nothing is contrary to Scripture. The kind of love Paul spoke about is love that acts, love that ministers, love that edifies. If we love our fellow believers, we will want to edify them. How do we edify them? With spiritual gifts. Why did Paul say, in 1 Corinthians 14:1, *"...but especially that you may prophesy"*? Because by prophesying we edify our fellow believers. By edifying them we express our love. If we sit there and do nothing for them, what is the good of telling them we love them?

In 1 Corinthians 13, Paul wrote about love for thirteen verses. Yet in 2 Corinthians 8 and 9, Paul wrote about money for thirty-nine verses. There are three times as many verses about money than there are about love. Does that mean money is more important than love? No. It means that if we love, one of the things we will do is use our money for God and for the people of God. If we keep speaking about love, but our money doesn't follow, we do not have very much love. More than that, we are deceiving ourselves. The same thing is true in the realm of the gifts of the Spirit. If we have love, we will desire to express this love by the exercise of spiritual gifts.

Truth #5:
If We Love God, We Receive His Gifts

If we love God, we will desire to receive and exercise His gifts to us. For example, can you imagine a mother making a beautiful birthday cake for her daughter, spending hours baking it, putting on the icing, and decorating it, and then when she brings it out, the girl saying, "Mommy, I love you, but I don't want your cake"? I don't think I have ever heard a child talk like that. It is really a denial of love. Or, imagine a young man who buys a beautiful diamond ring for the woman he loves and wants to marry. When he gives her the ring, if she says, "Honey, I love you, but I don't want your ring," it is unlikely they will ever get married.

It is not loving to reject the gift of the one whom we love. Likewise, it is not showing love for God when we refuse His gifts. If we think this way, we are deceiving ourselves. Matthew 7:11 says, *"If you then, being evil, know how to give good gifts to your children, how much more will your Father who is in heaven give good things to those who ask Him!"* In the almost identical verse in Luke 11:13, instead of *"give good things"* the text reads *"give the Holy Spirit."*

God has prepared spiritual gifts from eternity for our benefit.

Referring to our earlier analogy, imagine the little girl whose mother had baked the beautiful cake saying, "Well, Mother, I'm not sure the cake you baked is any good. Maybe you put something in it that will upset my stomach." What kind of a relationship does she have with her mother? Yet many Christians say to God, in effect, "These gifts of the Holy Spirit that are written about in Your Word—I do not really think they are of much use." This attitude is almost being irreverent. Some people say, "I'll have the baptism in the Holy Spirit, *even* if it means speaking in tongues." I do not want to criticize anything my heavenly Father has prepared from eternity for my benefit. If I do, I am being a very wayward child.

Let us look at one other passage. James wrote, *"Do not err* ["*be deceived*" NKJV], *my beloved brethren"* (James 1:16 KJV). I always wondered why he made that specific statement about not erring until one day I saw how it goes with the next verse. *"Every **good gift and every perfect gift** is from above, and comes down from the Father of lights, with whom there is no variation or shadow of turning"* (v. 17, emphasis added). God never gives you anything that is not perfect. Do not be under any misapprehension. If it comes from God, it is good.

If you are questioning the value or the worth of God's gift, you have a wrong picture of God. James said we are not to err or be deceived in this way. God's gifts are eminently to be desired, to be sought after. The more we love God, the more we will appreciate His gifts. If we turn down the gifts that have cost God so dearly the blood of His Son shed on the cross, we are grieving the Father's heart. We are grieving the Savior's heart, too.

Truth #6:
The Gifts Did Not End but Are Still for Today

Earlier, we talked about how some people believe the gifts ended with the early church. I have not found one suggestion in all of Scripture that the gifts were meant to end with the apostolic age. First, when did the apostolic age end? If the apostolic age lasts as long as there are apostles, then as far as I understand Scripture, this age is going to last until Jesus returns. Second, Paul wrote,

> *I thank my God always concerning you for the grace of God which was given to you by Christ Jesus, that you were enriched in everything by Him in all utterance and all knowledge, even as the testimony of Christ was confirmed in you, so that you come short in no gift, eagerly waiting for the revelation of our Lord Jesus Christ.*

> (1 Corinthians 1:4–7)

How long are the gifts to continue in the church? Until our Lord Jesus returns. The church that is waiting for the Lord Jesus is not to be lacking in any of the gifts. Notice what Paul said the gifts do: *"You were enriched in everything by Him."* A church without gifts is an impoverished church. Paul referred to the vocal gifts when he wrote, *"...enriched in...all utterance."* He referred to the gifts of revelation when he said, *"...enriched in...all knowledge."*

When the lame walk and the blind see, people know Jesus is there.

"Even as the testimony of Christ was confirmed in you." When the gifts are in operation—when the lame walk, the blind see, and gifts of revelation are exercised, people know Jesus is there; they know He is not a theory or a remote figure from the past but that He is still alive and is in the midst of His church. The testimony of Christ is confirmed.

Eagerly waiting for the revelation of our Lord Jesus Christ, who will also confirm you to the end, that you may be blameless in the day of our Lord Jesus Christ.

(1 Corinthians 1:7–8)

The above verses emphasize the fact that these gifts are to continue in the church right up to the coming of our Lord Jesus Christ at the end of the age. As a matter of fact, rather than suggesting the gifts will be withdrawn, the New Testament indicates they will become increasingly manifest as the age comes to its close.

And it shall come to pass in the last days, says God, that I will pour out of My Spirit on all flesh; your sons and

your daughters shall prophesy, your young men shall see visions, your old men shall dream dreams. And on My menservants and on My maidservants I will pour out My Spirit in those days; and they shall prophesy. I will show wonders in heaven above and signs in the earth beneath: blood and fire and vapor of smoke. The sun shall be turned into darkness, and the moon into blood, before the coming of the great and awesome day of the LORD.
(Acts 2:17–20)

This passage speaks of the day of the coming of the Lord Jesus Christ in glory and in power. It is clear the supernatural gifts spoken about here—prophecy, tongues, revelation, the whole picture of the supernatural operation of the Holy Spirit—are to continue and become increasingly manifest in the church as the age comes to its close. If they were already in the last days when Peter stood up and spoke on the day of Pentecost, how much more are we in the last days nearly two thousand years later? If the gifts are to be manifested in the church in the last days, and we believe we are right at the close of this age, then we should look for more and more of the gifts to be manifested. This is precisely what is happening. The gifts are being restored in an ever increasing measure almost daily in the days in which we are now living.

There is another reason for the increase of the operation of spiritual gifts in the church. Satan's power is going to increase. The closer we come to the end of the age, the more Satan is going to fight back, and the more he is going to seek to use and manifest his supernatural power through those who are the channels and instruments of what he seeks to do. Paul wrote in 1 Timothy 4:1, *"Now the Spirit expressly says that in latter times some will depart from the faith, giving heed to deceiving spirits and doctrines of demons."* Notice there is going to be an increasing activity of seducing religious spirits and demons bringing false doctrines within the church at the close of this age. How unreasonable it would be if God were to allow Satan to increase the power he manifests through his servants while decreasing the power He offers His people.

Then, in Paul's second letter to Timothy, he wrote,

But know this, that in the last days perilous times will come: For men will be lovers of themselves, lovers of money, boasters, proud, blasphemers, disobedient to parents, unthankful, unholy, unloving, unforgiving, slanderers, without self-control, brutal, despisers of good, traitors, headstrong, haughty, lovers of pleasure rather than lovers of God, having a form of godliness but denying its power. And from such people turn away! (2 Timothy 3:1–5)

We are going to see a great moral decline all around us at the close of this age. Some of the people who are going to experience this moral decline are religious people who have a form of godliness but deny its power. The power of true godliness is the power of the Holy Spirit. We are therefore warned against denying the presence and power of the Holy Spirit in the church at the close of this age.

In 2 Timothy 3:13, we are told, with reference to the close of the age, *"But evil men and impostors will grow worse and worse, deceiving and being deceived."* In the Greek, the word translated *"impostors"* refers to magicians or those who deliberately cultivate satanic powers. How much more then should Christians be endued with greater and greater power by the Holy Spirit?

Truth #7:
The Baptism and the Gifts Are Essential for Ministry

Jesus did not allow His own apostles to go out and begin to minister, preach, or take on any kind of service for Him, without His being present on earth, until they had been supernaturally endued with the power of the Holy Spirit. We have seen that, at the close of His earthly ministry, He said to His followers, *"Behold, I send the Promise of My Father upon you; but tarry in the city of Jerusalem until you are endued with power from on high"* (Luke 24:49). They were to wait in the city of Jerusalem until the promise of the Holy Spirit came upon them.

Recall that in Acts 1:8, Jesus gave the same warning in the last words He spoke before being taken up into heaven: *"But you shall receive power when the Holy Spirit has come upon you; and you shall be witnesses to Me in Jerusalem, and in all Judea and Samaria, and to the end of the earth."* He envisioned the gospel going forth to the ends of the earth always being propagated by the supernatural power of the Holy Spirit.

Truth #8:
The Gospel Is to Be Preached with "Signs Following"

God has ordained that the gospel should be preached with signs following. We read in the book of Mark,

[Jesus said,] *"Go into all the world and preach the gospel to every creature....And these signs will follow those who believe: In My name they will cast out demons; they will speak with new tongues; they will take up serpents; and if they drink anything deadly, it will by no means hurt them;*

they will lay hands on the sick, and they will recover." So
then, after the Lord had spoken to them, He was received up
into heaven, and sat down at the right hand of God. And
they went out and preached everywhere, the Lord working
with them and confirming the word through the accompany-
ing signs ["signs following" KJV].   (Mark 16:15, 17–20)

This is God's pattern. We are to preach the gospel, and
He will confirm the Word with signs following. Mark listed
five supernatural signs that will follow the preaching of the
gospel by believers and to believers. This preaching with signs
following is to continue until every creature has heard and the
gospel has been preached to the whole world. Since this has
not yet happened, the reason for the manifestation of the signs
has not yet ceased.

Remember how the gospel and accompanying signs were
demonstrated in the early church. In the ministry of Philip in
Samaria, the supernatural signs that accompanied his preaching were the attestation of his message.

Then Philip went down to the city of Samaria and preached
Christ to them. And the multitudes with one accord heeded
the things spoken by Philip, hearing and seeing the miracles
which he did. For unclean spirits, crying with a loud voice,
came out of many who were possessed; and many who were
paralyzed and lame were healed.   (Acts 8:5–7)

In Acts 28, when Paul and his company were shipwrecked
on the island of Malta, two supernatural signs arrested the
attention of the pagans in that area and opened them up to
the preaching of the gospel: Paul's immunity to the deadly
snakebite and the healing of Publius' father from fever and

dysentery, which also led to the healing of others on the island. It was not a lot of seminary training but the supernatural demonstration of the power of God that prepared the people to hear Paul's message. The same situation exists in the world today. In Romans 15:18–19, Paul said,

> *For I will not dare to speak of any of those things which Christ has not accomplished through me, in word and deed, to make the Gentiles obedient; in mighty signs and wonders, by the power of the Spirit of God, so that from Jerusalem and round about to Illyricum I have fully preached the gospel of Christ.*

What does it mean to fully preach the gospel of Christ? It means supernatural attestation by the power of the Holy Spirit with signs and wonders. What is the result of this supernatural attestation? It makes the Gentiles obedient. Again, I say this with a considerable amount of missionary experience. Without the demonstration of supernatural signs and wonders, you get only a certain measure of obedience—outward compliance with ceremonies and forms and requirements of a religious type, such as baptism and church membership. Yet with the supernatural power of God, which demonstrates people are dealing with a real and living God, comes real submission of hearts to Him. This is what changes people and makes them true disciples.

To fully preach the gospel of Christ means supernatural attestation with signs.

The writer of Hebrews gave three reasons why we should attend with great reverence to the gospel message:

THE *Gifts* OF THE SPIRIT

How shall we escape if we neglect so great a salvation, which at the first began to be spoken by the Lord, and was confirmed to us by those who heard Him, God also bearing witness both with signs and wonders, with various miracles, and gifts of the Holy Spirit, according to His own will? (Hebrews 2:3–4)

The gospel commands the serious attention of the human race for the following reasons. First, it began to be declared by the Lord Jesus Christ Himself. Second, it was recorded and handed down by those who heard Him personally, by those who were eyewitnesses. Third, God bears testimony to His Word with supernatural signs and gifts of the Holy Spirit. We have an obligation to present a gospel that is supernaturally attested by God if we demand complete obedience to God of those to whom we preach.

PRACTICAL INSTRUCTION FOR EXERCISING SPIRITUAL GIFTS

I would now like to give you some practical directions for moving forward in the realm of spiritual gifts.

Gifts Are to Function within a Body of Believers

First, the gifts of the Spirit are meant to function within an assembly of likeminded believers. We read in Matthew 5:15, *"Nor do they light a lamp and put it under a basket, but on a lamp-stand, and it gives light to all who are in the house."* In Revelation 1:20, the seven lampstands are designated as seven churches. In biblical times, lamps were filled with oil and ignited. If a lighted lamp was going to do any real good, it had to be placed on a lampstand. If you were to put it under a vessel of some kind, even though it was lighted, it would give no real light to the rest of the house.

Proverbs 20:27 says, *"The spirit of a man is the lamp of the Lord, searching all the inner depths of his heart."* The baptism in the Holy Spirit ignites the spirit of a person and sets it burning. Yet this is not sufficient. That ignited lamp must then be put in its correct place on the lampstand, which represents the church, the congregation, the body of Christ functioning together.

There will be a very definite limit to the measure in which you will truly operate in spiritual gifts if you are not rightly united to a group of believers who believe in and exercise the gifts. You will be frustrated, and eventually you will probably be quenched and become like a smoky vessel that once contained flames. You must get into fellowship with other believers who stand for the same truths and have received the same experiences. Then, the combined light of those individual lamps on the stand will really give light to all who are in the house. An essential requirement for correctly functioning in the gifts of the Spirit is therefore to be in fellowship with other believers who are likewise exercising these gifts.

Fellowship with other believers is essential for fully operating in the gifts.

Find Your Function in the Body

The second practical instruction is a very important point of order, which the apostle Paul brought out:

> *For as we have many members in one body, but all the members do not have the same function, so we, being many, are one body in Christ, and individually members of one*

another. Having then gifts differing according to the grace
that is given to us, let us use them: if prophecy, let us proph-
esy in proportion to our faith; or ministry, let us use it in our
ministering; he who teaches, in teaching; he who exhorts,
in exhortation; he who gives, with liberality; he who leads,
with diligence; he who shows mercy, with cheerfulness.

(Romans 12:4–8)

Paul listed various gifts we may operate in. Yet he said all believers do not have the same function. In order to fully exercise the gifts you have been given, you must find out what your function is in the body of Christ. God has a specific place for you in the body, a function for you to fulfill. If He has ordained you to be a hand, it is no good trying to operate as a foot because you will always be frustrated and will never really be effective.

We can find our function in the body through prayer for revelation and wisdom, by assessing our spiritual strengths and the areas in which we have a desire to serve, and by asking other believers to tell us how they already see us functioning in the body and where we are making contributions.

Another point we must recognize is that our function in the body of Christ is related to the faith God has given us. The Scripture tells us God has already given us a measure of faith. (See Romans 12:3.) If God intends you to be a hand, He will give you the faith needed to operate as a hand. He will not give you the faith needed to operate as a foot. People who are always struggling for faith are really advertising the fact that they are not in the right place in the body. With my physical body, my hand has no problem operating as a hand. It does so without a lot of bother or fuss; it is not a conscious effort. If I were to try to make my hand act like a foot, however, it would be an effort all the time. There would be frustration and strain because my hand was not intended for that. Again, where Christians are straining and ill at ease and continually struggling for faith, you can be sure they are not in the place in the body where they should be. They are not fulfilling their divinely appointed functions.

If you find your right function in the body, therefore, you will discover God has given you the proportion or measure of faith necessary to do that particular function. When you find your place, you will find the faith that goes with it. Our gift or gifts are often progressively manifested in our lives as we seek to obey God, through faith, in fulfilling our function in the body of Christ. These gifts correspond to our function and are needed to make us effective in it.

If you find your right function in the body, you will discover the faith you need.

For instance, if a man is called to be an evangelist, he may receive the gift of healing or the gift of miracles. If a man is called to be a prophet, he may receive the gifts of a word of wisdom, a word of knowledge, and discernings of spirits. If you do not discover your correct function, the right gifts may never operate in your life. Yet if you do discover your function, out of your faith will develop the operation of the gifts you need to function effectively.

Gifts Are Distributed according to God's Will

We must also remember that the distribution of the gifts is according to the will of God. First Corinthians 12:11 says, *"But one and the same Spirit works all these things, distributing to each one individually as He* [the Holy Spirit] *wills,"* and Hebrews 2:4 says, *"God also bearing witness both with signs and wonders, with various miracles, and gifts of the Holy Spirit, according to His own will."* We cannot set our will up in opposition to the will of God and say, "I will have this or that gift." *"For as many as are led by the Spirit of God, these are sons of God"* (Romans 8:14). If we want to live as children of God, we have to cultivate being led by the Spirit. This is a basic requirement of all Christian living. It applies to the operation of spiritual gifts as much as to anything else.

The Holy Spirit will reveal the specific gift or gifts He has given to us and may also direct us to exercise other gifts at particular moments of need. Even though we have already been given gifts according to the will of God, we can pray that these gifts will be revealed in our lives and that we would receive and manifest all the gifts the Spirit desires to give us.

While some people strive for gifts that are not theirs, others are more complacent and have the attitude of, "If God wills, He will give me a gift." If you have been saved for only a short time, God will listen to that. But if you have been saved several years and this is your attitude, it is often the result of laziness because at the end of that time, you should know much of the will of God as it is revealed in His Word. For example, we have seen there are certain gifts that are revealed in the Word of God to be His will for *all* believers. These are the gifts of tongues for private communion with God, and prophecy. Paul wrote, *"I wish you all spoke with tongues, but even more that you prophesied"* (1 Corinthians 14:5).

You could say this was just Paul's opinion. Yet shortly afterward, he wrote, *"If anyone thinks himself to be a prophet or spiritual, let him acknowledge that the things which I write to you are the commandments of the Lord"* (v. 37). Paul was not writing his personal opinion; he was writing by divine revelation with divine authority. This puts speaking with tongues and prophesying within the revealed will of God for all believers. We just need to pray for these gifts and move into the exercise of them.

Again, how many believers may prophesy? All. How many may speak with tongues? All. Those who are uncertain if it is God's will for them to receive a spiritual gift can be assured that speaking with tongues and prophesying are within the will of God for all believers—revealed in the supreme authority, which is the Word of God.

If You Ask, You Will Receive

When we pray for a spiritual gift, such as prophecy—the interpretation of tongues, or for another gift the Spirit is prompting us to exercise—we must receive it in faith, knowing that God will give what we ask. He gives us what is good, so we do not have to be afraid of asking.

In speaking about the baptism in the Holy Spirit, Jesus said,

> *So I say to you, ask, and it will be given to you; seek, and you will find; knock, and it will be opened to you. For everyone who asks receives, and he who seeks finds, and to him who knocks it will be opened. If a son asks for bread from any father among you, will he give him a stone? Or if he asks for a fish, will he give him a serpent instead of a fish? Or if he asks for an egg, will he offer him a scorpion? If you then, being evil, know how to give good gifts to your children, how much more will your heavenly Father give the Holy Spirit to those who ask Him!* (Luke 11:9–13)

As we have seen, in the parallel passage from Matthew 7, Jesus said, *"How much more will your Father who is in heaven give good things to those who ask Him!"* (v. 11).

While these passages refer to the baptism in the Holy Spirit, the principle they emphasize applies to whatever we ask of God, including individual gifts of the Spirit. We do not have to worry about what we will receive if we ask our heavenly Father for the gifts. Jesus said if you ask God for something good, will He give you something evil? The answer is never. If you ask for bread, what will He give you? Bread. If you ask for an egg, what will He give you? An egg. If you ask for a fish, what will He give you? A fish. If you ask for prophecy, what will He give you? Prophecy. This is the written guarantee in the Word of God that if you ask for a good thing according to God's Word, you will receive precisely what you ask for. Above all, remember if you ask for what is good, you will never receive what is evil.

If you ask for something good, God will never give you something evil.

If you bought a washing machine from Sears and there was a written warranty with it, you would not doubt for one moment you could go back to Sears and claim the fulfillment of that warranty. Every one of us has that much measure of faith in Sears. If many believers had half as much faith in God as they have in Sears, they would be moving in the realm of the gifts right now. It means taking God at His Word.

You Receive Right When You Ask

You may wonder when you will receive what you have asked for. The answer is you receive *when* you ask. *"Therefore I say to you, whatever things you ask when you pray, believe that you receive them, and you will have them"* (Mark 11:24). When do you receive them? When you pray. *"Now this is the confidence that we have in* [God], *that if we ask anything according to His will, He hears us. And if we know that He hears us, whatever we ask, we know that we have the petitions that we have asked of Him"* (1 John 5:14–15).

The devil always has a tomorrow. But the Bible says now is God's time. *"Now is the accepted time; behold, now is the day of salvation"* (2 Corinthians 6:2). If you listen to the devil's tomorrow, you will never enter into God's now. Suppose you ask for interpretation of tongues, and you receive it. What do you do? You give the interpretation. Of course, you do so within the parameters of an orderly assembly of believers, as we discussed earlier.

You may say, "I have never done it before. What if I don't say the right thing?" Ask yourself, "Did I ask for the right thing or for the wrong thing?" If the answer is the right thing, then ask yourself, "Did I believe I received it?" If you believed you received it, then, if you step out in faith, the right thing will come. How do you know? Because God promised. It does not come by what you feel, or by what somebody else says, but because God's Word declares if you ask for what is right, you will receive it. All you have to do after that is do it.

It is the same with prophecy and with anything you know to be within the revealed will of God according to His Word. When you ask for it, you receive it. When you receive it, you use it. If you do not use it, you will not have it. This is the order of faith.

Signs Follow Those Who Go

The next practical instruction is that signs follow those who "go." This relates to stepping out in faith to receive and exercise the gifts. We must not just understand the gifts in theory. We must do our part by being obedient to serve God and actively share our faith because this is way we will often see the gifts manifested through our lives. Jesus said to His disciples, *"**Go** into all the world and preach the gospel to every creature"* (Mark 16:15, emphasis added). After Jesus ascended to heaven, the disciples *"**went out** and preached everywhere, the Lord working with them and confirming the word through the **accompanying signs**"* (v. 20, emphasis added).

Believers are not to just sit in church; they are to go out and minister. If you park your car in the church parking lot and sit there for the rest of your life, how can anyone follow? You can only follow something that is moving.

Many times, people want to know what they should do to manifest spiritual gifts. Yet all they want to do is stay in church and sing hymns. You do not need any gifts for that. For centuries, people have been sitting in churches and never exercising any gifts. Many of the gifts of the Holy Spirit do not operate in a typical, institutional-type church service—even if the people are baptized in the Holy Spirit. They never see gifts of healing, they never hear a word of wisdom or a word of knowledge. I have been in churches where people have been baptized in the Spirit for twenty or thirty years but never once have seen the operation of any of the gifts beyond tongues, interpretation, and prophecy.

Yet in other settings, the gifts can thrive. I have seen young people travel to remote parts of the world, for example, with Youth With a Mission, and begin to evangelize. Remarkable miracles follow. Did they go to a Bible school to learn how to get miracles? No. They obeyed by going and ministering to others, and before they knew what was happening, the signs began to be manifested through their lives to meet the needs around them.

Signs follow those who go. If you want signs following, get ready to "go" and minister to others.

We Must Learn to Operate in the Gifts

Perhaps you are afraid you may make some mistakes in exercising the gifts. You would not be the first one. Almost everybody starts as a beginner in the exercise of spiritual gifts. If you want to begin perfect, do you know what will happen? You will never begin at all.

Exercise your spiritual gifts. If you make a mistake, God will pick you up.

If you do make a mistake, that's all right. God will pick you up. The Bible says the righteous man falls seven times but God picks him up eight times. (See Proverbs 24:16.) He does not remain on the ground; he remains up. Remember Paul's words, *"You can all prophesy one by one, **that all may learn and all may be encour-**

aged" (1 Corinthians 14:31, emphasis added). There is such a thing as learning the exercise of spiritual gifts. Hebrews 5:14 tells us maturity comes by having our senses exercised. If we never exercise, we will never mature. To learn to exercise the gifts, you need to be in a group of believers who love you, are patient with you, and do not suppress you but encourage you.

We Must Check Our Motives

Finally, when you have come this far, double-check your motives. The right motive for operating in the spiritual gifts is that the church may be edified. *"Even so you, since you are zealous for spiritual gifts, let it be for the edification of the church that you seek to excel"* (1 Corinthians 14:12).

EQUIPPED FOR EVERY GOOD WORK

As we conclude this study of the gifts of the Spirit, I would like to encourage you, as Paul encouraged Timothy,

Continue in the things which you have learned and been assured of....All Scripture is given by inspiration of God, and is profitable for doctrine, for reproof, for correction, for instruction in righteousness, that the man of God may be complete, thoroughly equipped for every good work.

(2 Timothy 3:14, 16–17)

The gifts of the Spirit will help equip you for every good work, to the edification of the church and the salvation of the world.

About the Author,
Derek Prince

Derek Prince (1915–2003) was born in Bangalore, India, into a British military family. He was educated as a scholar of classical languages (Greek, Latin, Hebrew, and Aramaic) at Eton College and Cambridge University in England and later at Hebrew University, Israel. As a student, he was a philosopher and self-proclaimed atheist. He held a fellowship in ancient and modern philosophy at King's College, Cambridge.

While in the British Medical Corps during World War II, Prince began to study the Bible as a philosophical work. Converted through a powerful encounter with Jesus Christ, he was baptized in the Holy Spirit a few days later. This life-changing experience altered the whole course of his life, which he thereafter devoted to studying and teaching the Bible as the Word of God.

Discharged from the army in Jerusalem in 1945, he married Lydia Christensen, founder of a children's home there. Upon their marriage, he immediately became father to Lydia's eight adopted daughters—six Jewish, one Palestinian Arab, and one English. Together, the family saw the rebirth of the state of Israel in 1948. In the late 1950s, the Princes adopted another daughter while Derek was serving as principal of a college in Kenya.

In 1963, the Princes immigrated to the United States and pastored a church in Seattle. Stirred by the tragedy of John F. Kennedy's assassination, he began to teach Americans how to intercede for their nation. In 1973, he became one of the founders of Intercessors for America. His book *Shaping History through Prayer and Fasting* has awakened Christians around the world to their responsibility to pray for their governments. Many consider underground translations of the book as instrumental in the fall of communist regimes in the USSR, East Germany, and Czechoslovakia.

Lydia Prince died in 1975, and Derek married Ruth Baker (a single mother to three adopted children) in 1978. He met his second wife, like his first, while he was serving the Lord in Jerusalem. Ruth died in December 1998 in Jerusalem, where they had lived since 1981.

Until a few years before his own death in 2003 at the age of eighty-eight, Prince persisted in the ministry God had called him to as he traveled the world, imparting God's revealed truth, praying for the sick and afflicted, and sharing his prophetic insights into world events in the light of Scripture. He wrote more than fifty books, which have been translated into more than sixty languages and distributed worldwide. He pioneered teaching on such groundbreaking themes as generational curses, the biblical significance of Israel, and demonology.

Derek Prince Ministries, with its international headquarters in Charlotte, North Carolina, continues to distribute his teachings and to train missionaries, church leaders, and congregations through its worldwide branch offices. Prince's radio program, *Keys to Successful Living* (now known as *Derek Prince Legacy Radio*), began in 1979 and has been translated into more than a dozen languages. Estimates are that Derek Prince's clear, nondenominational, nonsectarian teaching of the Bible has reached more than half the globe.

Internationally recognized as a Bible scholar and spiritual patriarch, Derek Prince established a teaching ministry that spanned six continents and more than sixty years. In 2002, he said, "It is my desire—and I believe the Lord's desire—that this ministry continue the work, which God began through me over sixty years ago, until Jesus returns."

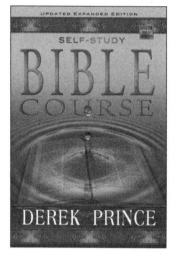

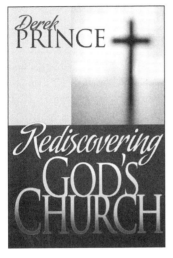
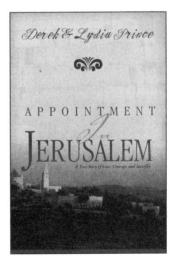

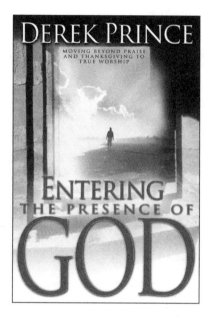

Entering the Presence of God:
Moving Beyond Praise and Thanksgiving to True Worship
Derek Prince

"The harder I try to be good, the worse off I am!" If that sounds like you, there's good news. Internationally acclaimed Bible teacher Derek Prince shows the way to victorious intimacy with God as he explains how you can enter into His very presence to embrace the spiritual, physical, and emotional blessings of true worship. Learn the secrets of entering into His rest, fellowshipping with the Lord, receiving divine revelation from God's Spirit, and conducting spiritual warfare. Discover how to be freed from the bondage of guilt and sin and obtain an inner peace and joy that nothing else can duplicate. Don't miss out on the thrill of worship…God's way!

ISBN: 978-0-88368-719-2 • Trade • 176 pages

WHITAKER
HOUSE

www.whitakerhouse.com